Fearon Teacher Aids a division of **Pitman Learning, Inc.,** Belmont, California

I.M.A. BOOKSNOOP'S
Amazing · Astounding · Astonishing

Library Skills Kit

ELAINE PRIZZI and JEANNE HOFFMAN

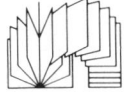

MAKEMASTER® Blackline Masters

Editorial director: Roberta Suid
Editors: Bonnie Bernstein and Kate Fuller
Text and cover designer: Wendy Calmenson
Illustrator: Duane Bibby
Design manager: Susan True
Production editors: Robert E. Wanetick and Mary McClellan
Manufacturing manager: Susan Fox

Entire contents copyright © 1983 by Pitman Learning, Inc., 19 Davis Drive, Belmont, California 94002. Member of the Pitman Group. Permission is hereby granted to reproduce designated materials in this book for noncommercial classroom and individual use.

ISBN-0-8224-2253-0
Printed in the United States of America.

1.9 8 7 6 5 4 3 2

CONTENTS

Introduction, 3
Booksnoop Pretest, 6

UNIT 1: Alphabet Sleuth 9

MOTIVATIONAL RIDDLES The Organizers, 10
BULLETIN BOARD Clarence Croaker and the Croakettes, 10
GAME Alphabet Sentences, 12
TRANSPARENCY MASTER How to Be a Detective, 13
DUPLICATING MASTERS Alphabet Clues, 14 • Name Sleuth, 15 • The Detective's Assistant, 16 • Investigating Guide Words, 17 • Guide Word Graduate, 18 • Alphabet Sleuth Test, 19

UNIT 2: Parts of a Book 20

MOTIVATIONAL RIDDLES Four Parts, 21
BULLETIN BOARD All About Books, 22
GAME Book Look, 23
TRANSPARENCY MASTER There Are Two Sides to Every Story: The Title Page, 24
DUPLICATING MASTERS Sifting for Big Clues: The Table of Contents, 25 • Sifting for Clues: Using the Index, 26 • The Informer: The Bibliography, 28 • Parts of a Book Test, 29

UNIT 3: The Dewey Decimal System 31

MOTIVATIONAL RIDDLE Where, Oh Where, Has My Little Book Gone? 32
BULLETIN BOARD I. M. A. Booksnoop's Fallen Shelves, 32
GAME Dewey Decimal Relay, 34
TRANSPARENCY MASTER Where Is It? 35
DUPLICATING MASTERS Following Leads, 36 • Looking for Clues, 37 • Remembering the Clues, 38 • Dewey Decimal System Test, 39

UNIT 4: The Card Catalog 40

MOTIVATIONAL RIDDLE It's in the Cards, 41
BULLETIN BOARD Catalog These Bees, 41
GAME Card Catalog Fish, 43
TRANSPARENCY MASTER Tracing the Cards, 44
DUPLICATING MASTERS Tracing the Trays, 45 • Clues in the Trays, 46 • Clues in the Cards, 47 • Unscramble the Clues, 48 • Card Catalog Test, 49

UNIT 5: The Thesaurus 50

MOTIVATIONAL RIDDLE One to Nine, 51
BULLETIN BOARD Theo Saurus, 51
GAME Do You Understand? 53
TRANSPARENCY MASTER Crime Stopper, 54
DUPLICATING MASTERS Sailing by Thesaurus, 55 • Finding the Rhyme for Us Using a Thesaurus, 56 • The Thesaurus Goes to the Movies, 57 • Thesaurus Test, 58

UNIT 6: **The Atlas** 59

    MOTIVATIONAL RIDDLE Exploring, 60
    BULLETIN BOARD Atlas Match, 60
    GAME Westward, Ho! 62
    TRANSPARENCY MASTER Your Travel Guide: The Atlas, 63
    DUPLICATING MASTERS Getting Acquainted, 64 • Making Conversation, 65 • Being Neighborly, 66 • Atlas Test, 67

UNIT 7: **Bartlett's Familiar Quotations** 68

    MOTIVATIONAL RIDDLE Meet Mr. Bartlett, 69
    BULLETIN BOARD Match the Pears, 69
    GAME Bart-ades, 71
    TRANSPARENCY MASTER Meet Mr. Bartlett, 72
    DUPLICATING MASTERS Getting in Step with Bartlett, 73 • Who Said That? 74 • The Case of the Interrupted Quotation, 75 • Bartlett's Test, 76

UNIT 8: **The Almanac** 77

    MOTIVATIONAL RIDDLE Department Store for Questioners, 78
    BULLETIN BOARD Elapsed Events, 78
    GAME Categories—Nobel Awards, 80
    TRANSPARENCY MASTER Using the Fact Locator, 81
    DUPLICATING MASTERS Which Department? 82 • Department, Please! 83 • Only the Facts, Please! 84 • Almanac Test, 85

UNIT 9: **The Encyclopedia** 86

    MOTIVATIONAL RIDDLE Can You Find It? 87
    BULLETIN BOARD I'm in a Pickle! 87
    GAMES Verify the Facts, 89 • Encyclopedia Categories, 90
    TRANSPARENCY MASTER Finding the Keys, 91
    DUPLICATING MASTERS Using the Keys, 92 • Who Did It? 93 • Discover the Details, 94 • Encyclopedia Test, 96

UNIT 10: **The Biographical Dictionary** 97

    MOTIVATIONAL RIDDLE He Spread Light, 98
    BULLETIN BOARD World's Most Wanted Wonderful Winners, 98
    GAME Unscramble, 100
    TRANSPARENCY MASTER Biographical Dictionary Page, 102
    DUPLICATING MASTERS Who Am I? 103 • Aliases, 104 • How Are We Related? 105 • Biographical Dictionary Test, 106

UNIT 11: **The Geographical Dictionary** 107

    MOTIVATIONAL RIDDLE A Popular Name Game, 108
    BULLETIN BOARD Where Is It? 108
    GAME From Last to First, 110
    TRANSPARENCY MASTER Geographical Dictionary Page, 111
    DUPLICATING MASTERS Finding Your Way, 112 • Clues from First to Last, 113 • Get the Geographical Facts, 114 • Geographical Dictionary Test, 115

Teacher's Notes and Answer Keys, 116

INTRODUCTION

Welcome to *I. M. A. Booksnoop's Amazing, Astounding, Astonishing Library Skills Kit.* Everything you need to open up the world of the library and books to your students is right here between these two covers. Materials are conveniently arranged in units and include duplicatable worksheets featuring our supersleuth, I. M. A. Booksnoop, who is there to help you and your students investigate the library system and some books on the reference shelf. Here's what the kit contains:

- A statement of objectives and classroom-management suggestions for each unit.
- Blackline masters for student worksheets that develop skills needed to use the library and seven useful reference books. The worksheets are adaptable to grades 5 through 8.
- Blackline masters for a pretest and unit mastery tests.
- A blackline transparency master for each unit to help introduce new skills.
- Motivational riddles to spark interest in each unit.
- Games for each unit designed to reinforce new skills.
- Interactive bulletin board ideas that provoke initial student interest and involvement in each unit.
- A Teacher's Notes section providing a statement of objectives, suggestions for use, and an answer key for the worksheets.

Unlike other kits, *I. M. A. Booksnoop's Amazing, Astounding, Astonishing Library Skills Kit* offers flexibility and economy. Multiple worksheets are offered in each unit, so you can select what you need for your particular teaching situation. The duplicatable masters prevent you from wasting money on fancy items that can be used only once. Each page is perforated, allowing it to be easily and cleanly detached. But best of all, everything—absolutely *everything*—you need is conveniently packaged between these covers.

We strongly believe that books open new worlds for our students. That's why we want our students to experience the library as a friendly and accessible place. One way is to help them become familiar with specialized reference books—the library's tools for learning.

We also believe that increased time spent on tasks increases learning and retention, and we have designed our worksheets accordingly. Moreover, we have made each worksheet a self-contained activity that students can work on without supervision to further develop their independent work habits.

How to Use This Kit

How do you use *I. M. A. Booksnoop's Amazing, Astounding, Astonishing Library Skills Kit?* It's elementary! I. M. A. Booksnoop's prescription for motivating and improving your students' library skills is totally adaptable to your teaching needs. First, administer the pretest to determine your students' current skill levels. Then, adjusting for what your time and energy budget allow, this is what your teaching plan for a typical unit should be:

- Display I. M. A. Booksnoop's poster and the riddle to spark initial interest in the unit.
- Make and present the unit transparency to introduce a new skill.
- Duplicate the worksheets you want to use.
- Collect the necessary reference books.
- Intersperse student work periods with the correlated game.
- Construct the companion bulletin board to reinforce and extend the concepts.
- Administer the mastery test.
- Consult the Suggestions for Use section at the beginning of the unit for more ideas.

Meet the Detective, I. M. A. Booksnoop

Our detective, I. M. A. Booksnoop, will spark your students' interest in books. The Booksnoop poster and the unit riddles are designed to introduce the topics. Here's how to enlarge the I. M. A. Booksnoop poster on page 1.

MATERIALS
- posterboard or other good-quality paper
- overhead projector
- felt-tip pen
- scissors

PROCEDURE

1. Use a thermofax machine to make a transparency of the I. M. A. Booksnoop poster on page 1, or trace the design onto an overhead transparency.

2. Decide what size you want the poster to be and cut the posterboard accordingly.

3. Project the transparency and trace the poster outlines onto the posterboard with a felt-tip pen. Color the poster or invite your students to color it if you wish.

Display the finished poster with an appropriate riddle at the beginning of each unit. Here are directions for using the poster and riddles in conjunction with each unit.

MATERIALS
- enlarged I. M. A. Booksnoop poster
- piece of paper to fit inside magnifying glass on poster
- unit riddle
- pen
- pushpin

PROCEDURE

1. Print the riddle on the piece of paper.

2. Attach the riddle to the magnifying glass in the Booksnoop poster.

3. Explain to your group how you wish them to present their answers (orally or in written form).

4. Change the riddle at the beginning of each new unit.

NAME _____

Booksnoop Pretest

A. Alphabetical Order: Number the words in each list below in alphabetical order.

1. ___ winter
   ___ trust
   ___ fragile
   ___ canary
   ___ staple

2. ___ dairy
   ___ deed
   ___ down
   ___ draft
   ___ diner

B. Guide Words: The guide words for a page in a reference book are *pirate* and *Pluto*. Circle the words below that would be found on the page.

1. private   3. pleat   5. pistol   7. plastic
2. plate   4. piracy   6. plot   8. purple

C. Choosing Key Words: Circle the key word or words in each question below that you would look up in an index or an encyclopedia to find the answer to the question.

1. Who invented the camera?
2. What foods were eaten by the early Pueblo Indians?
3. Did Alexander the Great conquer the Egyptians?
4. Who was the first doctor to use antibiotics?
5. What products are manufactured in Alabama?

NAME _____

Booksnoop Pretest continued

D. Using the Library: Write *true* or *false* next to each sentence below.

_____ 1. All books in a library are arranged in alphabetical order.

_____ 2. The card catalog has three cards for each book in the library.

_____ 3. Encyclopedias and almanacs are found in the reference section of the library.

_____ 4. The Dewey Decimal System uses numbers and alphabetical order to classify books.

_____ 5. Fiction books are listed in the 800s in the Dewey Decimal System.

E. Choosing Reference Books

a. almanac
b. atlas
c. biographical dictionary
d. book of quotations
e. encyclopedia
f. geographical dictionary
g. thesaurus

Write the letter of the reference book above that would be the *best* help in answering each question below.

___ 1. What are the parts of a flower?

___ 2. Who won the Kentucky Derby last year?

___ 3. Who said, "One if by land . . ."?

___ 4. What is the area of Alaska?

___ 5. What is the capital city of Ethiopia?

___ 6. When did Thomas Jefferson live?

___ 7. Which countries border France?

___ 8. What books did Mark Twain write?

___ 9. What is another word for *cloudy*?

___ 10. What languages are spoken in India?

Booksnoop Pretest 7

NAME _____

Booksnoop Pretest *continued*

F. Using Reference Books: Write *true* or *false* next to each sentence below.

_____ 1. The table of contents is the fastest way to find a topic in a book.

_____ 2. A bibliography can tell you where to find more information.

_____ 3. To find out more about Charles Lindbergh, use Volume C of an encyclopedia.

_____ 4. An atlas has an alphabetical index of place names.

_____ 5. The biographical dictionary gives facts about famous people.

_____ 6. An almanac is published yearly.

_____ 7. The geographical dictionary will give you all the facts you need for a report about Japan.

_____ 8. A thesaurus lists synonyms (and sometimes antonyms) for many words.

_____ 9. Some encyclopedias have indexes.

_____ 10. A book of quotations lists all the sayings of an important person.

Unit 1

Alphabet Sleuth

Objective

The students will review and strengthen their alphabetizing skills and their abilities to use guide words.

Before You Begin

Use the alphabetical order and guide word sections of the pretest to determine which students will benefit from the activities in this unit. Knowledge of the alphabet and efficient use of guide words are prerequisites to success with the materials in *Booksnoop*.

Motivational Riddles
The Organizers

SUGGESTIONS FOR USE Use these riddles to introduce the alphabet and guide words as valuable tools for the quick and efficient use of reference books. Attach a riddle to the magnifying glass in the Booksnoop poster (see page 1).

RIDDLE #1

I am the organizer. I am the key!
When you use a reference book, you need me.
I'm easy to spot: *Z* is my bottom and *A* is my top.
I am the _____, you see.
   Answer: Alphabet

RIDDLE #2

When you use a reference book, it's me you should heed.
I'm on every page, and my job is to lead.
I'm always the first, and I'm always the last.
If you use me, you will find things fast!
   Answer: Guide words

Bulletin Board
Clarence Croaker and the Croakettes

OBJECTIVE The pupils will practice alphabetizing.

DESCRIPTION Various song titles and names of members of a singing group are placed in alphabetical order.

SUGGESTIONS FOR USE Use this bulletin board to review and reinforce the topics covered in Unit 1.

MATERIALS
- tagboard, 21 inches by 26 inches, seven or eight sheets in various colors
- scissors
- felt-tip pen
- pushpins
- hole punch

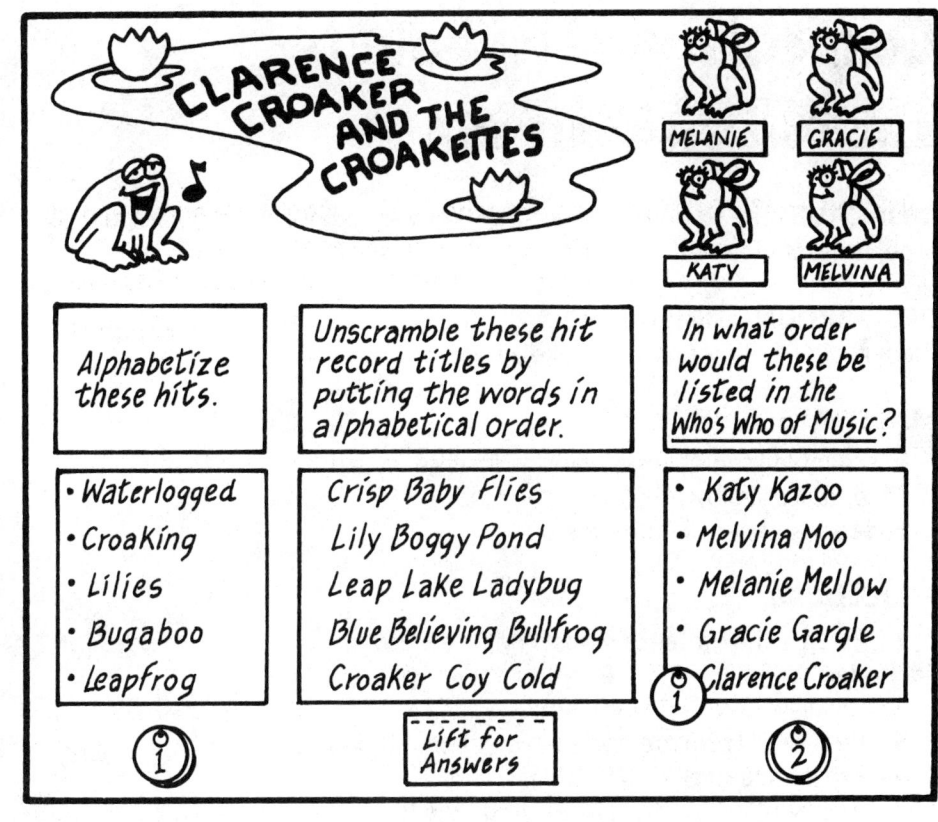

PROCEDURE

1. Cut a lily pad and lilies out of the tagboard. Print the title on the lily pad. Staple the lily pad and lilies to the board.

2. Draw a pattern and cut out four female frogs. Staple them to the board.

3. Reverse the pattern that was used for the female frogs (omit the bow) and use it for Clarence. Trace and cut out Clarence and staple him to the board.

4. Cut four rectangles out of tagboard for the Croakettes' names. Print the names and staple them to the board.

5. Cut three more rectangles out of tagboard. Print the directions on them and staple them to the board.

6. Cut three more rectangles out of tagboard. Print the items to be alphabetized on them and staple them to the board.

7. Position pushpins next to each of the hits to be alphabetized and each name in the *Who's Who in Music* list.

8. Cut 10 circles and number the circles from 1 to 5 twice. Suspend each set of circles from a pushpin positioned under the hits and *Who's Who* lists. The pushpins hold the circles when they are not being used.

9. Print the answers on a piece of tagboard and staple it so that they will be exposed when the bottom edge of the paper is lifted.

Alphabet Sleuth 11

Game
Alphabet Sentences

OBJECTIVE The students will use their knowledge of alphabetical order to organize sentences.

DESCRIPTION Teams compete to be the first to unscramble words and put them in alphabetical order to make a sentence.

MATERIALS
- scrambled sentences on tagboard sentence strips (see the sample sentences below)
- paper and pencil for each student

PROCEDURE
1. Prepare the sentence strips. Print the answers on the reverse sides for easy reference.
2. Divide your group into teams.
3. Be sure all team members have paper and pencil.
4. Explain the rules:
    a. The object of the game is to be the first team to unscramble the words by putting them in alphabetical order to make a sentence.
    b. When the sentence is written in alphabetical order on the players' papers, the players raise their hands. The teacher will ask the first player who raised a hand to read the unscrambled sentence.
    c. One point is scored for each correctly unscrambled sentence.
    d. If the player incorrectly unscrambled the words, the teacher will ask the next player who raised a hand, and so on.
    e. When all the sentences are unscrambled, the team with the highest score wins.

SAMPLE SCRAMBLES

Scrambled great Charles honor elephants drew for.
Unscrambled Charles drew elephants for great honor.

Scrambled skippers salvage sailors spy scrap sixteen scarce since secretly stealthily.
Unscrambled Sailors salvage scarce scrap secretly since sixteen skippers spy stealthily.

TRANSPARENCY MASTER

How to Be a Detective

A. Alphabetizing: Circle the word in each pair below that would come first in a reference book. Underline the letter that tells you.

1. Alabama *or* Alamo?
2. motorcycle *or* motorcade?
3. rhinoceros *or* rhinestone?
4. coaster *or* coast guard?
5. microbiology *or* microbe?

B. Names: Circle the name in each pair below that would come first in a reference book.

1. Alice Baker *or* Andrew Bailey?
2. Smith, John *or* Samuel, Aaron?
3. Mount Everest *or* Montevideo?
4. Amazon River *or* Mississippi River?
5. George Washington Carver *or* George Washington?

C. Guide Words: Tell whether each word below comes *before*, *on*, or *after* the page on which these guide words appear.

salamander   sassafras

_____ 1. sable
_____ 2. stable
_____ 3. Sahara
_____ 4. sandpiper
_____ 5. saucer

_____ 6. stalactite
_____ 7. Saturn
_____ 8. Salome
_____ 9. San Juan
_____ 10. Saskatchewan

Alphabet Sleuth 13

NAME _____

Alphabet Clues

A. The most useful piece of equipment in your detective kit is the alphabet. Show how well you know the alphabet. Write the next three letters of the alphabet that follow each letter listed below.

1. b ___ ___ ___   5. s ___ ___ ___   9. e ___ ___ ___

2. m ___ ___ ___   6. w ___ ___ ___   10. u ___ ___ ___

3. d ___ ___ ___   7. c ___ ___ ___   11. h ___ ___ ___

4. l ___ ___ ___   8. i ___ ___ ___   12. p ___ ___ ___

B. Once you know the alphabet, it is easy to put words in alphabetical order. Number the words in each list below in alphabetical order. In the second list, look at the second letter of each word to determine the alphabetical order. In the third list, look at the third letter in each word.

1. ___ menace   2. ___ coffee   3. ___ frail

   ___ apple   ___ cite   ___ freeze

   ___ simple   ___ camper   ___ friend

   ___ detour   ___ cube   ___ frond

   ___ value   ___ cellar   ___ fruit

C. Sometimes you will have to look at the fourth, the fifth, or even the sixth letters to decide which word comes first. Underline the word in each pair below that comes first in alphabetical order. Circle the letters in the words that help you decide.

1. straight *or* strange   6. cyclone *or* cycle
2. Pluto *or* plutonium   7. whale *or* wheat
3. Egypt *or* egoism   8. rodent *or* rodeo
4. mosaic *or* mosque   9. video *or* victory
5. Alabama *or* Alamo   10. brazen *or* Brazil

14 I. M. A. Booksnoop

NAME _____

Name Sleuth

A. A detective must be able to locate names quickly, too! Names are placed in alphabetical order using the last names. Number the names below in alphabetical order.

___ Cornwall, James   ___ Hogan, James

___ Johnson, Gerald   ___ Taylor, Samuel

___ Solomon, Susan   ___ Preston, Harry

___ Adams, June   ___ Gordon, Arthur

___ Jackson, Edith   ___ Richards, John

B. Don't be fooled when the name is written the way we normally say it—for example, *Thomas Adams.* You still use the last name to determine the alphabetical order. Number the names below in alphabetical order.

___ Ann Harrison   ___ Andrew Beckwith

___ Joel Newman   ___ Ronald Levin

___ Albert Smith   ___ George Romaldi

___ Scott Perry   ___ Charles Moore

___ Patricia Newhouse   ___ Barbara Caldwell

C. If the last names are the same, then the first names are used to determine alphabetical order. Number the names below in alphabetical order.

___ John Smythe   ___ Wilson Calhoun

___ Jerry Smythe   ___ Sally Talbot

___ Sara Talbot   ___ Julia Wilson

___ Jack Berens   ___ Jane Berens

___ Lyle Calhoun   ___ Lisa Lyons

Alphabet Sleuth 15

NAME _____

The Detective's Assistant

Guide words are the detective's assistant. Most reference books use guide words to help you find entries more quickly. There are two guide words at the top of each page. By looking at the guide words, you can decide whether the word you are looking for would be on that page. Here is a sample of two guide words for a page and some of the words that would be found on the page.

camp   **candle**
campaign   Canada
camphor   Canada goose
camporee   canal

Camp is the first word on the page and *candle* is the last word listed on the page. The words listed on the page all come alphabetically between *camp* and *candle*.

A. The guide words for a page are *marble* and *Marie Antoinette*. Circle the words in the list below that would be found on the page.

Marianas Islands	market	Manchuria
music	mammoth	March
Maria Theresa	mare	Mecca
McKinley	monsters	manganese
neutron	Marburg	margarine

B. Use your own words to tell what guide words are.

_____

_____

16   I. M. A. Booksnoop

NAME _____

Investigating Guide Words

Guide words will tell you where to go to find the entry you want. If your word comes alphabetically before the first guide word, then you know you need to look closer to the front of the book. If the entry you want comes after the second guide word, then you know you need to turn toward the back of the book.

A. The guide words for a page are *Paris* and *Pompeii.* Tell whether each word in the list below comes before, on, or after the page. Write *before, on,* or *after* next to each word.

_____ 1. Plato   _____ 6. Poland

_____ 2. Panama   _____ 7. Peking

_____ 3. Prussia   _____ 8. Pueblo

_____ 4. Pikes Peak   _____ 9. Pacific

_____ 5. Persia   _____ 10. Pontiac

B. The guide words for a page are *Cascade* and *Cleopatra.* Circle the names in the list below that would be found on the page.

1. Clay, Henry   6. Cabot, John
2. Cape Town   7. Charles I
3. Cicero   8. Cato
4. Carroll, Charles   9. Clark, George R.
5. Churchill, Winston   10. Cleveland, Grover

C. Renumber the names in part B in alphabetical order.

Alphabet Sleuth 17

NAME _____

Guide Word Graduate

A. The guide words for a page are *Salem* and *Scotland*. Circle the words in the list below that would be found on the page.

1. Santiago
2. Sahara
3. Siberia
4. Santa Fe
5. Saigon
6. Sidney
7. Scilly Isles
8. Scranton
9. Sonora
10. Scipio
11. Schubert, Franz
12. Saxony

B. The guide words for a page are *chevron* and *Chile*. Tell whether each word in the list below comes before, on, or after the page. Write *before, on,* or *after* next to each word.

_____ 1. Chicago
_____ 2. cheese
_____ 3. chrome
_____ 4. child
_____ 5. chetah
_____ 6. chimney
_____ 7. chieftain
_____ 8. chicle
_____ 9. Cheyenne
_____ 10. chlorine
_____ 11. Chickasaw
_____ 12. chic
_____ 13. chemical
_____ 14. chipmunk
_____ 15. checkers
_____ 16. Chief of Staff

C. Rewrite the words in part B in alphabetical order below.

_____ _____ _____ _____
_____ _____ _____ _____
_____ _____ _____ _____
_____ _____ _____ _____

18 I. M. A. Booksnoop

NAME _____

Alphabet Sleuth Test

A. Number the words or names in each list below in alphabetical order.

1. ___ shelf
   ___ shed
   ___ sew
   ___ shatter
   ___ sheep
   ___ shave
   ___ shimmer
   ___ shock

2. ___ John Bates
   ___ Thomas Becket
   ___ Sarah Bates
   ___ Andrew Brown
   ___ Carl Bering
   ___ Benjamin Bell
   ___ Betsy Brown
   ___ Susan Byron

B. The guide words for a page are *Washington* and *Windsor*. Circle the names in the list below that would be found on the page.

1. Winchester
2. Weddell
3. Wales
4. Wisconsin
5. Warsaw
6. Virginia
7. Westchester
8. Whitehorse
9. West Indies
10. Wyoming
11. Waterford
12. White Nile
13. Washington
14. Winnipeg

Alphabet Sleuth 19

Unit 2

Parts of a Book

Objective

The students will become familiar with the functions of the title page, the table of contents, the index, and the bibliography section and will be able to locate information in these sections of a book.

Before You Begin

Use part F of the pretest to determine whether students need to strengthen their knowledge of the parts of a book, then choose the appropriate activities. Introduce these activities by having the students leaf through fiction and nonfiction books and locate and name the parts of a book that are not part of the text. See page 118 in the Teacher's Notes section for a complete explanation of the parts of a book.

Motivational Riddles
Four Parts

SUGGESTIONS FOR USE Use these riddles to introduce this unit and to motivate the appropriate lessons. Attach a riddle to the magnifying glass in the Booksnoop poster. Use the first riddle as a group motivator and the other riddles as contests.

RIDDLE #1

You might look at me for the book name
Or the book title; it's all the same.
The illustrator you might discover
By using these clues plus another:
At the beginning I usually sit.
Guess what I am to score a hit!
   Answer: Title page

RIDDLE #2

Near or at the end you will find me,
I'm more than one page, usually!
The topics in a book I tell,
I will help you if you use me well.
Look with some care, and you'll find me soon!
   Answer: Index

RIDDLE #3

I am the names of some books in a book.
You can find me — take a look!
The alphabet helps to keep me in line.
As a source of more facts, I'm a real gold mine.
Near the end you will most often find me.
Just unlock the clues by using this key!
   Answer: Bibliography

RIDDLE #4

After the title but before the index,
After the table of contents but before the appendix,
I give credit where credit is due . . .
Another name for a simple thank you.
   Answer: Acknowledgements

Bulletin Board
All about Books

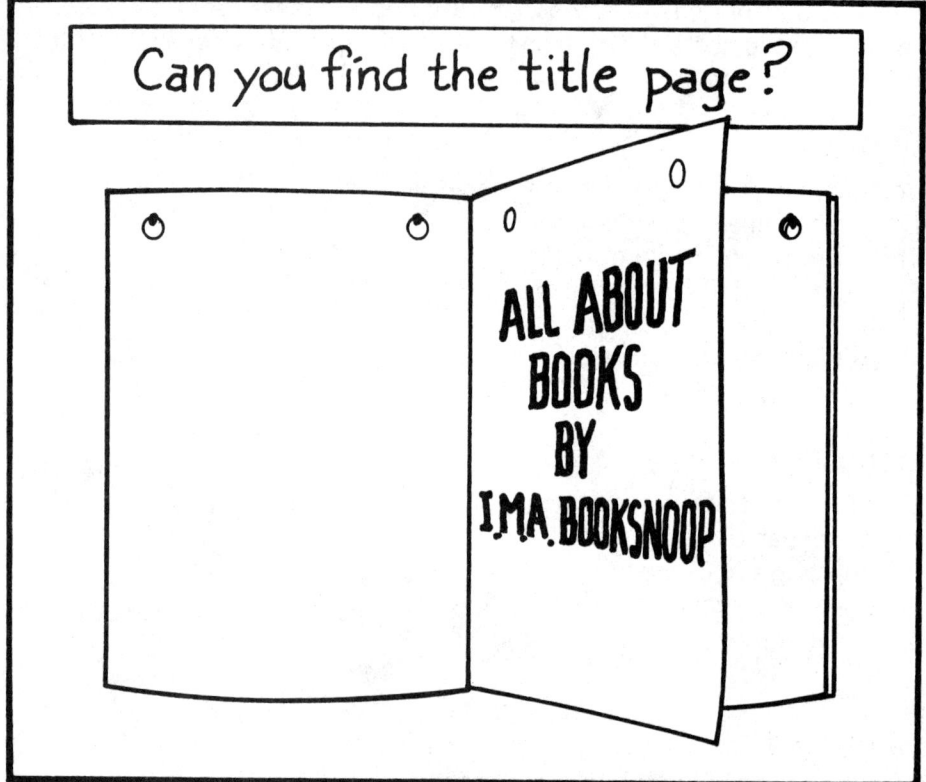

OBJECTIVE The students will locate the parts of a book.

DESCRIPTION A larger-than-life book is manipulated to illustrate the various parts of a book.

SUGGESTIONS FOR USE Use this bulletin board to introduce the topics you wish to cover in Unit 2. If you plan to discuss parts of a book not covered by the duplicating masters, use this bulletin board to present them.

MATERIALS
- tagboard, 21 inches by 26 inches, three or more sheets
- transparent tape
- hole punch
- pushpins
- construction paper
- pen
- stapler

PROCEDURE

1. Tape two sheets of tagboard together along the 26-inch edge. Tape additional sheets for each part of a book you wish to present to your group.
2. Punch two holes in the top edge of each sheet, about 2 inches down from the top and 2 inches in from the outside edges. Make the holes large enough to fit easily over the head of a pushpin.
3. Use a classroom book as your model. Print a sample page for each part of a book you wish to present — title page, table of contents, index, and so on.
4. Print a challenge on a piece of construction paper: "Can you find the _____?" Staple it in position on the bulletin board.
5. Position two pushpins on the bulletin board, matching the distance between the holes in the book.
6. Position two more pushpins to hold the book when the pages are open. The holes in the book should rest on the heads of the pushpins. This will allow the pages of the book to be turned easily.

Game
Book Look

OBJECTIVE The students will match the information found in various parts of a book with the names of the parts.

DESCRIPTION This is a teacher-directed game. You may organize competition for team or individual play.

SUGGESTIONS FOR USE Use this game as a review.

MATERIALS

- sheet of notebook paper and pencil for each player or each team
- teacher-prepared information statements

PROCEDURE

1. Prepare information statements by listing information that would be found in various parts of a book.
2. Divide your group into teams, if desired, and provide paper and pencil.
3. Explain the rules to your group:
    a. The object of the game is to complete your game sheet.
    b. Prepare your game sheet by listing any five parts of a book. Skip a line after each part.
    c. An information statement will be read. Write the information under the correct heading. If the statement is "Written by Irene Hunt," write it under Title Page, because this is where you would find it.
    d. The first person or team to complete a sheet is the winner.
    e. Make a new game sheet and we will try again.

TRANSPARENCY MASTER

There Are Two Sides to Every Story: The Title Page

Read this title page and its other side. Then use the information to answer the questions below.

Title Page	Other Side
Land of Many Cultures by Eric Dalton Illustrated by Margaret Batesford Fairfield Publishers New York	Copyright © 1975 by Fairfield Publishers All rights reserved. Printed in the United States of America. ISBN 0-603-02437-1

1. Who wrote the book? _____

2. What is the title? _____

3. Who published the book? _____

4. Where was it published? _____

5. Who illustrated the book? _____

6. What is the date of copyright? _____

7. Is the information in the book current enough to be used for a report? _____ Why or why not? _____

8. What is the International Standard Book Number (ISBN)? _____

I. M. A. Booksnoop

Sifting for Big Clues: The Table of Contents

A. Answer the questions about a table of contents below.

1. Where will you find it in any book? _____

2. Which does it tell you — the main ideas found in the book or the details? _____

B. Read the table of contents below. Then answer the questions.

Indians of Central America

1.	Early Peoples in Central America	4
2.	The Beginnings of Agriculture	27
3.	The Lost Civilization of the Mayas	32
4.	The Toltecs of Mexico	68
5.	The Rise of the Aztecs	82
6.	The Coming of the Explorers	114
7.	Cortez the Conqueror	127
8.	The Spanish Influence	134
9.	The Indians Today	142
10.	The Outlook for the Future	155
	List of Illustrations and Maps	161
	Glossary	163
	Index	192

1. What is the title of Chapter 5? _____

2. How many chapters are listed? _____

3. Which chapter would tell you about the changes the Spanish brought? _____

4. Which chapter would tell you about the foods grown by Indians in Central America? _____

5. Where would you look to find out how to pronounce Tenochtitlan? _____

6. Where would you look if you wanted to know if the book had information about the Mixtecs? _____

NAME _____

Sifting for Clues: Using the Index

Use the section of the index below to answer the questions on these two worksheets.

gauchos, 79, 82*
government, 129–135
    Argentina, in, 189
    Bolivia, in, 64
    Chile, in, 70
    collective farms, 80
    economic system and, 130
    Paraguay, in, 72
    political parties, 131
Guatemala, 92–93

*illustration

Guyana, 90
Havana, 25
Incas, 50–55
    capital, Cuzco, 50
    farming methods, 52*
    government, 50
    location, 50
    mining, 54
    Spanish conquest, 55
Indians, 35–60

astronomy, 40
Aztecs, 40–45
    Brazil, in, 46
    cities, 40, 50
    food, 36, 42
    homes, 36, 42
    Incas, 50–55
    languages, 41, 47
    Mayas, 55–60
    religion, 42, 47, 58
    temples, 42,* 47, 49,* 58, 60*

A. Use the index to answer the questions below. On what page or pages would you find:

_____ 1. information about Brazilian Indians?

_____ 2. a picture of a gaucho?

_____ 3. the names of Indian languages?

_____ 4. the way the Incas farmed?

_____ 5. pictures of Indian temples?

_____ 6. the form of government in Bolivia?

_____ 7. what the Indians knew about astronomy?

B. Pretend you are an index maker. Number the entries below in the order in which they would appear in an index.

___ Lake Titicaca, 4

___ Mayas, 55–60

___ Isthmus of Panama, 15

___ Jamaica, 10

___ Lake Maracaibo, 4

___ industry, 20

___ Magellan, F., 65

___ currency, 38–39

26 I. M. A. Booksnoop

NAME _____

Sifting for Clues: Using the Index *continued*

C. Use the index to answer the questions below. You may need to look under more than one heading.
On what page or pages might you find:

_____ 1. what foods the Incas ate?

_____ 2. the religions of the Indians?

_____ 3. the results of the Spanish conquest?

_____ 4. the important buildings?

_____ 5. a picture of an Inca Indian?

_____ 6. who has the right to vote in Argentina?

_____ 7. what crops are grown in Guatemala?

D. Answer the questions about indexes below.

1. How are the items in an index arranged?
   _____

2. How does an index save time?
   _____

3. How may an index tell you there is a picture of the item you are interested in? _____

4. What does a dash between two page numbers mean?
   _____

5. Why is an index better than a table of contents for finding items in a book? _____

Parts of a Book 27

NAME _____

The Informer: The Bibliography

A. Use this sample bibliography to answer the questions below.

Allred, Calvin, *Life of the Aztecs.* Boston: Purlman Publishers, 1978.
Caulfred, Henry, *Latin American Governments.* London: Atman, 1976.
Emery, Stephen, *Incas of the Andes.* New York: Smithfield Publishers, 1980.
Frankfort, Jonathan, *Spanish Conquerors.* New York: Lockman and Sons, 1976.
Hayman, Frederick, *Art and Architecture of the Mayas.* New York: Robertson Press, 1979.
Lernan, Alan, *The Story of Latin American Independence.* Boston: Edwards and Sons, 1970.

1. Would a bibliography be in the front, the middle, or the back of a book? _____

2. How can a bibliography help you? _____
_____
_____

3. In what order are books listed in a bibliography? _____
_____

B. Use the bibliography above. Write the last name of the author of the book or books that would:

1. have a picture of a Mayan temple. _____

2. tell you which country or countries have presidents. _____

3. probably have out-of-date information. _____

4. tell you about the Indians of Latin America. _____
   _____   _____

5. tell you how the Spanish treated the Indians. _____

6. be the most up-to-date. _____

7. tell you about the ways the Indian chiefs governed.
   _____   _____

NAME _____

Parts of a Book Test

A. Match each part of a book listed below with the type of information it may give you. Write the letters in the blanks. You may use a letter more than once.

Information **Part**

___ 1. Author's name   a. Title page
   b. Table of contents
___ 2. List of chapters   c. Copyright page
   d. Index
___ 3. Copyright date   e. Bibliography

___ 4. Location of an illustration

___ 5. Books the author used as sources for facts

___ 6. The International Standard Book Number

___ 7. Books for finding more information

___ 8. Publisher's name

___ 9. Exact location of an item

___ 10. Illustrator's name

B. Read each statement below. Write *true* or *false* next to each one.

_____ 1. The title page tells you the main topics in a book.

_____ 2. The table of contents lists the chapters in the order you would find them in the book.

_____ 3. You can use the index to locate items quickly.

_____ 4. The bibliography lists the copyright dates of the books the author used.

_____ 5. The index is in alphabetical order.

NAME _____

C. Use this section of index to answer the questions below. There may be more than one answer to a question.

Inca empire, 28–56
  achievements, 55–56
  cities in, 34
  communication, 29, 32–35
  date of, 28
  extent of, 28
  farming, 30–33
  government, 37–42
  language of, 28
  population, 28
  Spanish conquest, 43–45
  transportation, 32
  travel in, 29, 32–35
  unexplained mysteries, 55
India, 189–235
  achievements, 230–235
  caste system, 210–213
  farming, 192–195
  industry, 196–203
  land use, 203
  population, 189–191
  religions, major, 204–212
  social structure, 210–213

1. Which pages will tell you whether the Incas had a king or a chieftain? _____

2. Which pages would you look at to find out whether the Incas built roads? _____

3. Which pages would help you find out what the local foods of India are? _____

4. Under what other topic heading could you look to find out about the caste system? (Which topic appears on the same four pages as the caste system?) _____

5. On which pages would you look for a map showing the crops grown in India? _____

6. Where would you look to find information about the buildings the Incas left? _____

7. Where would you look to find the important manufacturing centers in India? _____

8. Where would you look to find out about irrigation channels built by the Incas? _____

I. M. A. Booksnoop

Unit 3

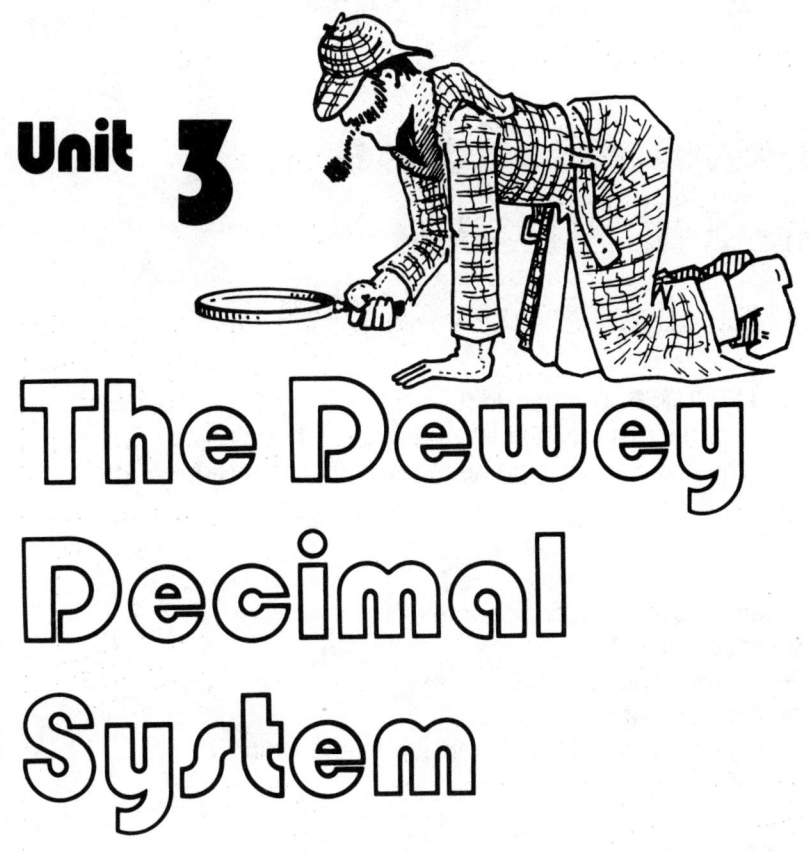

The Dewey Decimal System

Objective

The students will become familiar with the Dewey Decimal System.

Before You Begin

Your library may use the Library of Congress system rather than the Dewey Decimal System for cataloging and shelving books. If so, you will need to revise the numbers on Unit 3's worksheets accordingly.

Motivational Riddle
Where, Oh Where, Has My Little Book Gone?

SUGGESTION FOR USE Use this riddle as a follow-up to your teaching. Attach the riddle to the magnifying glass in the Booksnoop poster. Change the third line of the riddle as appropriate to review other portions of the Dewey Decimal System.

RIDDLE

Where, oh where, has my little book gone?
Where, oh where can it be?
I need it to learn how to play a game.
Oh where, oh where can it be?
  Answer: 700s, Arts, games, music, dancing, and painting

Bulletin Board
I. M. A. Booksnoop's Fallen Shelves

OBJECTIVE The students will use the Dewey Decimal System to classify a given set of book titles.

DESCRIPTION The students' task is to sort book cards according to their Dewey Decimal System categories. Change the book cards to update this board quickly. Increase the level of difficulty as your students' skills develop.

MATERIALS

- six sheets of tagboard of assorted colors
- I. M. A. Booksnoop poster art, page 1
- scissors
- pen
- stapler
- construction paper

PROCEDURE

  1. Reproduce I. M. A. Booksnoop by following the steps on page 5. Staple him to the bulletin board.
  2. Cut out a dialogue balloon large enough to accommodate the following message: "I'm in trouble! All of my books have fallen from my

shelves. Can you put them in order? Place the correct number, section name, and books on each of the shelves. Thank you!" Staple the balloon to the bulletin board.

3. Make the shelves. Cut strips of tagboard 1½ inches wide. Staple them to the bulletin board along their lower edges. Make as many shelves as will fit on your bulletin board; space the shelves about 1 inch farther apart than the height of your books.

4. Cut ten 3-by-4-inch cards. Print a Dewey Decimal System number at the top of each card so that the number shows when the card is placed in the shelf. (See page 37 for the Dewey Decimal System classification chart.)

5. Cut ten 3-by-6-inch cards. Print a Dewey Decimal System classification name at the top of each card so that the name shows when the card is placed in the shelf strip.

6. Cut a 2-by-7-inch strip for each book title you wish to use. Print a title on each strip. Use five to seven books for each category.

7. Use three pieces of 8½-by-11-inch construction paper to make three storage pockets. Fold up the bottom third of each sheet and staple along the edges, forming a pocket. Label one pocket Numbers, one pocket Sections, and one pocket Books. Staple the pockets to the bulletin board.

8. Print an answer key on a piece of construction paper. On a matching piece of construction paper, print Answer Key. Cover the answers with this piece of paper and staple along the top only. This makes a flap that can be lifted by the students to check their work.

Game
Dewey Decimal Relay

OBJECTIVE The students will use the Dewey Decimal System to classify books.

DESCRIPTION Teams compete to be the first to correctly classify a list of book titles.

MATERIALS

- game sheet listing the Dewey Decimal System numbers and categories for each team. (See page 37 for this list.)
- lists of book titles

PROCEDURE

1. Prepare the game sheets. Every time a new game is played, a new game sheet is required for each team.
2. Prepare lists of 10 book titles. A new list is needed for each game.
3. Decide how you wish to present the book title lists — on the chalkboard, on chart paper, or on an overhead projector — and prepare them accordingly.
4. Divide your group into teams.
5. Explain the rules:
    a. The object of the game is to be the first team to complete a correct list of book titles according to the Dewey Decimal System.
    b. The first player writes a title from the master list next to the correct category and then passes the game sheet and pencil to the next player.
    c. The second player must write a different title next to a different category, and so on.
    d. If a player finds an error made by a team member, the player may correct it.
    e. The last player stands when finished.
6. Give the first player on each team a game sheet and a pencil, reveal the book title list, and give the signal to start.

TRANSPARENCY MASTER

Where Is It?

A. Nonfiction: Which topics are represented by these Dewey Decimal System numbers?

1. 000–099 _____

2. 100–199 _____

3. 200–299 _____

4. 300–399 _____

5. 400–499 _____

6. 500–599 _____

7. 600–699 _____

8. 700–799 _____

9. 800–899 _____

10. 900–999 _____

B. Fiction: Number the books below in the order in which they would be arranged in a library.

___ *Benjy Goes to Town,* by Sara Jackson

___ *Benjy Finds a Thief,* by Sara Jackson

___ *Ben and His Motorcycle,* by Anne Adamson

___ *Betsy Buys a Bike,* by John Callahan

___ *Albert Is Always Late,* by Alan Waters

The Dewey Decimal System

NAME _____

Following Leads

In detective work, a lead is a clue. The Dewey Decimal System can give you leads to interesting reading by telling you where to find topics in the library. Here are some facts about the Dewey Decimal System:

1. The system groups nonfiction books by topic.
2. Each topic has a number.
3. Fiction books are arranged by the author's last name.
4. Each book has a call number that is its "address" in the library.

Browse through each Dewey Decimal System section in your library. Look for leads and follow them to interesting books. Find a book that interests you in each section. Fill in the chart below so that you can find the book quickly when you want to read it.

Section	Call Number	Title and Author
000–099	_____	_____
100–199	_____	_____
200–299	_____	_____
300–399	_____	_____
400–499	_____	_____
500–599	_____	_____
600–699	_____	_____
700–799	_____	_____
800–899	_____	_____
900–999	_____	_____
Fiction A–H	_____	_____
Fiction I–O	_____	_____
Fiction P–Z	_____	_____

Good detectives check out their leads! Follow up your leads by reading the books you listed.

I. M. A. Booksnoop

NAME _____

Looking for Clues

Knowing where items belong will help you find clues. Read the Dewey Decimal System classification chart below. Then read the title of each book listed below. Decide which Dewey Decimal System category each book belongs to. Write the number of the category in the blank.

Dewey Decimal System Classification Numbers

000–099 General Works (encyclopedias, references)
100–199 Philosophy (ideas about behavior, thought, knowledge, nature, and psychology)
200–299 Religion (all religions of all time)
300–399 Social Sciences (education, law, civics)
400–499 Language (languages, grammar, etymology)
500–599 Pure Science (biology, chemistry, physics)
600–699 Technology (applied science, home, industry)
700–799 Arts (music, painting, sculpture, games)
800–899 Literature (poetry, plays, and books about literature)
900–999 History (biography, geography, history of civilizations)

_____ 1. *Story of the Alphabet,* by Edward Clodd

_____ 2. *Life in Colonial America,* by Edith Speare

_____ 3. *Roads,* by Jon W. Boardman

_____ 4. *All About Stars,* by Anne T. White

_____ 5. *The First Book of the Olympic Games,* by John Welsh

_____ 6. *Laughable Limericks,* by Sara and John E. Brown

_____ 7. *The First Book of the Constitution,* by R. B. Norris

_____ 8. *Skateboarding,* by Howart Reiser

_____ 9. *The Magic of Music,* by Lorrain E. Watters

_____ 10. *Familiar Quotations,* by John Bartlett

_____ 11. *Gods and Heroes,* by Sally Benson

_____ 12. *The Republic,* by Plato

The Dewey Decimal System 37

NAME _____

Remembering the Clues

An easy way to remember facts is to make a *mnemonic* device — something to help you remember. For example, you can use the first letters of the facts you want to remember as the first letters of the words in a sentence. Do you know the names of the lines of the G clef in music? They are: "Every good boy does fine" — e, g, b, d, f.

A. Suppose you need to remember the planets in order of increasing size. They are: Mercury, Pluto, Mars, Venus, Earth, Neptune, Uranus, Saturn, and Jupiter. Use the first letter of each planet's name to complete the mnemonic sentence below.

___echanics ___repare ___any ___enus ___xpeditions,

___ever ___sing ___trange ___alopies.

B. Try making your own mnemonic device to help you remember the Dewey Decimal System categories in order. The categories are: General, Philosophy, Religion, Social Sciences, Language, Science, Technology, Arts, Literature, and History. Write your words in the blanks below. Then write out your complete mnemonic sentence.

g_____   p_____   r_____

s_____   l_____   s_____

t_____   a_____   l_____

h_____

_____

_____

38 I. M. A. Booksnoop

NAME _____

Dewey Decimal System Test

Match each book title below with the Dewey Decimal System category it belongs in. Write the first number of the category in the blank next to the title.

Dewey Decimal System

000–099	General Works	500–599	Pure Science
100–199	Philosophy	600–699	Technology
200–299	Religion	700–799	Arts
300–399	Social Sciences	800–899	Literature
400–499	Language	900–999	History

Book Titles

_____ 1. *The History of New York City*

_____ 2. *French for Beginners*

_____ 3. *New Games for Large Groups*

_____ 4. *Hinduism, the Ancient Religion*

_____ 5. *Being and Nothingness*

_____ 6. *All About Computers*

_____ 7. *The Scientific Dictionary*

_____ 8. *Poems to Make You Laugh*

_____ 9. *The Art of the Navahos*

_____ 10. *Paul Revere Rides Again*

Unit 4

The Card Catalog

Objective

The students will become familiar with the card catalog and the three types of information cards used in a card catalog.

Suggestions for Use

The ability to use the card catalog efficiently makes finding a book much easier. Periodically review the skills in this section, since they are probably the most useful to library users.

Motivational Riddle
It's in the Cards

SUGGESTION FOR USE Use this riddle to stimulate interest in the card catalog. Attach the riddle to the magnifying glass in the Booksnoop poster. Challenge your students to make up their own riddles that can be answered with a book title.

RIDDLE
A nonfiction book I am, that is true.
To find me is the thing you must do.
Mischievous I am, my title does say.
I'm about a raccoon that likes to play.
A direction is my author's last name.
Sure hope you can find me and win the game!
　Answer: Rascal, by Sterling North

Bulletin Board
Catalog These Bees

DESCRIPTION The students will sort catalog cards by type—author, subject, or title.

MATERIALS
- construction paper, brown and yellow
- tagboard, brown and yellow
- black felt-tip pen
- stapler
- hole punch
- pushpins
- discarded library catalog cards from the *B*s or blank index cards to make your own

PROCEDURE
　1. Prepare the caption Catalog These Bees, then staple it in position on the bulletin board.
　2. Make three beehives from yellow or light brown construction paper. Label them Subject, Author, and Title.
　3. Use yellow tagboard and a black felt-tip pen to make a bee for each catalog card you have collected or made.
　4. Staple each catalog card to the body of a bee. Punch a hole in the top of each bee (avoiding the printing on the card). The hole must be large enough to accommodate the head of a pushpin.

5. Make a storage pocket for the bees. Fold a piece of construction paper up one third. Staple the outside edges to form a pocket.

6. Print an answer key on a piece of construction paper. Cover it with another piece of construction paper labeled Answer Key, and staple it at the top to make a flap.

7. Print the following directions on a piece of construction paper:

Catalog These Bees

1. Put the catalog cards in the correct hives.
2. Lift the flap to check your answers.
3. Return the bees to the storage pocket when finished.

8. Staple the components in position on the bulletin board. Place the number of pushpins needed for each type of card beneath each hive. The cards rest on the plastic part of the pushpin.

Game
Card Catalog Fish

OBJECTIVE The students will match the author, title, and subject cards for a book.

DESCRIPTION The familiar game of "Go Fish" makes matching the author, title, and subject cards an enjoyable way to learn to recognize the three types of cards.

MATERIALS
- 51 blank cards cut to playing card size *or* 17 sets of discarded catalog cards

PROCEDURE

  1. Prepare the playing cards. If your librarian does not have old cards to give you, print author, title, and subject cards for 17 books.

  2. Place a copy of the following game directions at the game table:

Card Catalog Fish
1. Two to six people may play.
2. The cards are shuffled, and six cards are dealt to each player.
3. The remaining cards are placed face down in the center of the table.
4. The player on the right of the dealer goes first.
5. The player asks the person on the right for an author, subject, or title card but does not specify for which book. If the player on the right has the kind of card requested, he or she must surrender it. If the player does not have the requested card, a card is drawn from the pile. Play moves to the right.
6. When all three cards for a book are collected, the player lays them down and gets an extra turn.
7. The player who makes the most sets of three cards is the winner.

  3. Increase the difficulty of the game by using cards featuring the same subject or similar titles.

TRANSPARENCY MASTER

Tracing the Cards

Use the information below to make three catalog cards for the book.

Winning at Tennis   Brownsville Publishers 1982   176p illus.   Erica Gonzales   Illus by Janet Winslow.   786 G   TENNIS

1.

Type of card: _____

2.

Type of card: _____

3.

Type of card: _____

NAME _____

Tracing the Trays

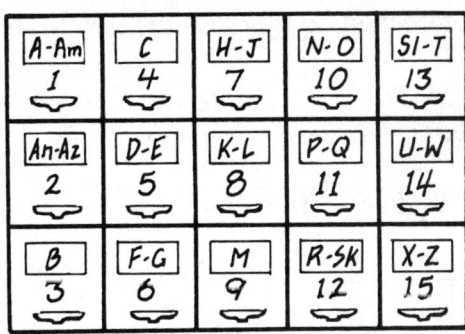

A. For each book below, write the number of the catalog card tray above that would hold the title card for the book.

_____ 1. *What Animal Is It?,* by Anna Pretorius

_____ 2. *All About Birds,* by Robert Lemmon

_____ 3. *A Midsummer Night's Dream,* by William Shakespeare

_____ 4. *Adventures with the Heroes,* by Catherine F. Sellew

_____ 5. *The Buildings of Ancient Egypt,* by Helen Leacroft

B. For each book below, write the number of the catalog card tray above that would hold the subject card for the book.

_____ 1. *Carlsbad Caverns* _____ 5. *Treaty of Utrecht*

_____ 2. *Malaria* _____ 6. *Seashells*

_____ 3. *Hundred Years' War* _____ 7. *Map Making*

_____ 4. *Sir Lancelot* _____ 8. *Rodents*

C. For each book below, write the number of the catalog card tray above that would hold the author card for the book.

_____ 1. *The Susquehanna from New York to Chesapeake,* by Elizabeth Carmer

_____ 2. *Sixth Sense,* by Larry Kettlekamp

_____ 3. *Rip Van Winkle and the Legend of Sleepy Hollow,* by Washington Irving

_____ 4. *My Village in Greece,* by Sonia and Tim Gidel

_____ 5. *White Horses and Black Bulls,* by Alan C. Jenkins

The Card Catalog 45

NAME _____

Clues in the Trays

A. Explore any card catalog tray. Use the tray to complete each sentence below.

1. My tray number is _____ .

2. It contains entries beginning with _____ and ending with _____ .

3. Four guide words used in this tray are _____ , _____ , _____ , and _____ .

B. Follow the instructions to answer each question below.

1. Find an author card. What information is on the first line of the card?
   _____

   How many books by that author are indexed in your catalog tray? _____

2. Find a title card for a fiction book. What is the title of the book?
   _____

3. Find a title card for a nonfiction book. What is the title of the book?
   _____

4. Find two titles that begin with the same word. What are the titles?
   _____ and _____

5. Find cards for two nonfiction books. What are the call numbers?
   _____ and _____

6. Find a subject card. What is the heading on the card?
   _____ . How many books are listed under this heading? _____

NAME _____

Clues in the Cards

A. Use this catalog card to answer the questions below.

```
636.7     DOGS
  Mc      McCloy, James
              Dogs at work.   Illus by Sheila Beatty.
          Crown 1979      74p illus.
```

1. Type of card? _____

2. What is the book's call number? _____

3. What part of the call number identifies the author? _____

B. Use this catalog card to answer the questions below.

```
293
  C       Closse, Robert
              Odin and his family.   Illus by Betty Clark.
          Crisfield Publishers 1970    120p illus.
```

1. Type of card? _____

2. What is the title of the book? _____

3. Who wrote the book? _____

C. Use this catalog card to answer the questions below.

```
          Mystery at lochearn hill
          Kasner, Lawrence
              Mystery at lochern hill.   Illus by George Knobb.
          Scoson Publishers 1972     94p illus.
```

1. Type of card? _____

2. Where in the library would you find the book? _____

3. Who drew the pictures for the book? _____

The Card Catalog 47

NAME _____

Unscramble the Clues

Use the "clues" below to make three catalog cards for the book.

Life in ancient egypt	Scribner Publishers 1975
164p illus.	Illus by Marg. Boehmer.
Kenneth Fowler	932 F
EGYPT

1. Subject card

2. Title card

3. Author card

48 I. M. A. Booksnoop

NAME _____

Card Catalog Test

A. Name the three types of cards in a card catalog.

_____ _____ _____

B. Use this catalog card to answer the questions below.

```
            AMERICAN HISTORY
976.6
   A     Abbott, Sarah H.
             The gold rush days.   Illus by Jane Soo.
         Goldstone 1965         172p illus.
```

1. What is the title of the book? _____

2. Who is the author? _____

3. When was the book copyrighted? _____

4. What is its call number? _____

5. Who is the publisher? _____

C. Use the information below to make a title card for the book.

Mystery of the missing computer   138p illus.
Nancy Morrison   Weldon Publishing 1983
Illus by Jerry Smith.

_____

The Card Catalog   49

Unit 5

The Thesaurus

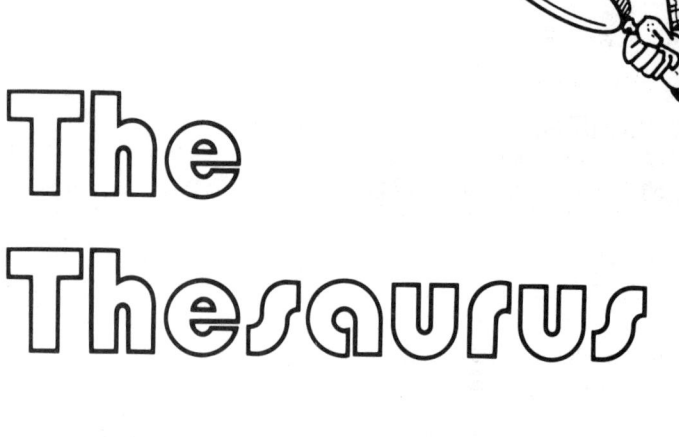

Objective

The students will use a thesaurus to find synonyms for given words and will learn its value as a tool for better writing.

Suggestions for Use

Everyone will benefit from browsing through a thesaurus. Challenge your more able students to find more than one substitute word. Encourage students to share interesting words they find. Make charts of words that can be substituted for those overworked words you are so tired of reading in compositions: *nice, happy, beautiful, good,* and so forth.

Motivational Riddle
One to Nine

SUGGESTIONS FOR USE Use this riddle after you have introduced the thesaurus. Attach the riddle to the magnifying glass in the Booksnoop poster. Encourage your students to make up riddles of their own that follow this pattern.

RIDDLE
My first is in lame, but not in pale.
With my second and fourth you can see my third and fifth.
My third is in name, but not in game.
My fifth is like a snake.
My sixth is one hundred.
My seventh falls between t and v.
Although I have an eighth and ninth,
No further clues will I give you.
Just look in your thesaurus under *small*,
And you will know the name to call!
   Answer: Miniscule

Bulletin Board
Theo Saurus

OBJECTIVE The students will use the thesaurus to find synonyms for overworked words.

DESCRIPTION Our favorite dinosaur, Theo Saurus, asks your students to change his spots by finding new words for those worn-out favorites.

MATERIALS
- construction paper, three or more colors
- felt-tip pen
- stapler
- scissors
- ditto master
- compass or saucer

PROCEDURE
 1. Make Theo Saurus from construction paper. Staple him in position on the bulletin board.
 2. Prepare the caption and print the speech balloon, using construction paper for both. Staple them in position on the bulletin board.

3. Using a saucer or a compass, make a ditto master for Theo's spots. Print Name and Old Word on one circle and New Word on another. Run the ditto master on construction paper and cut out the circles.

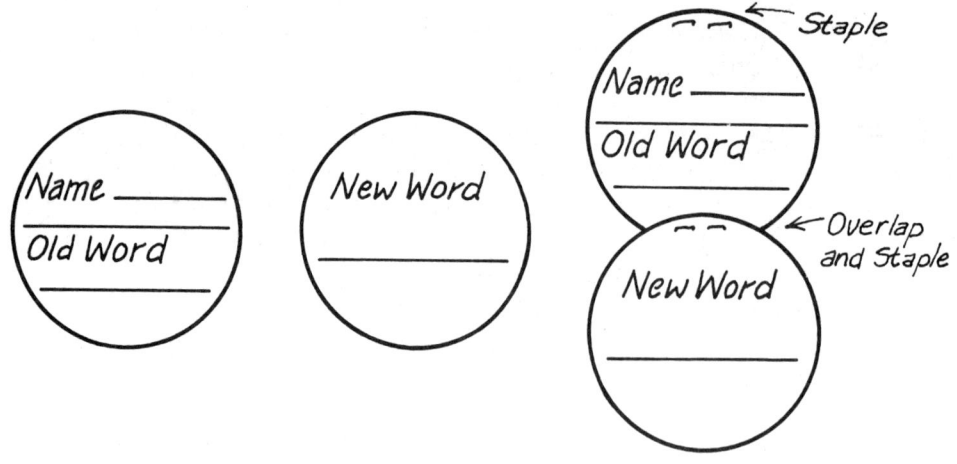

4. Make a storage pocket by folding a piece of construction paper up one third and stapling along the edges. Label the pocket New Spots and staple it in position on the bulletin board. Place the new-word spots and a felt-tip pen in the pocket. Make another pocket, labeled Old Spots. Place the old-word spots and a felt-tip pen inside.

5. Cut out six more circles and print an overused word on each one. Position the circles on Theo.

6. Print the following directions on a piece of construction paper. Then staple the paper in position on the bulletin board.

Change Theo's Spots

1. Find a word on Theo that you use too often when you write.
2. Use the thesaurus to find an interesting synonym for your overused word.
3. Take an old spot and a new spot and fill in the blanks.
4. Show your new spot to your teacher and ask for the stapler. Staple your new spot to the board so that it overlaps the old spot.

Game

Do You Understand?

OBJECTIVE The students will use the thesaurus to rewrite familiar material.

DESCRIPTION Teams compete to stump each other with translations of familiar sayings and titles.

MATERIALS

- at least one thesaurus for each team
- game list for each team

PROCEDURE

1. Prepare the game lists, each with five titles or sayings. For example, use five television show titles, five book titles, five song titles, or five proverbs.

2. Divide your group into three or more teams.

3. Explain the rules of the game:

    a. The object of the game is to earn the most points by preparing the translations and using them to stump the other teams.

    b. Each team will be given a game sheet.

    c. Use the thesaurus to translate the material on the game sheet. (*Read the examples below.*) The first team to complete the translations earns five points, the second earns three points, and the third, one point. (*Adjust the scoring if you have more than three teams.*)

    d. Each team will challenge the others to guess the original material.

    e. Each time you stump another team, your team will earn a point.

EXAMPLES

1. "Birds of a feather flock together" becomes "Fowl of similar plumage congregate collectively."

2. "Star Wars" becomes "Conflict Among the Celestial Bodies."

3. "Rock Around the Clock" becomes "Circular Transit About the Chronograph."

TRANSPARENCY MASTER

Crime Stopper

The thesaurus, or dictionary of synonyms, is a crime stopper. It will help you avoid the crime of using the same old words over and over. Read this sample index from a thesaurus.

shock, *v.* surprise 407
   upset 692
   repel 579, 617
shocking horrible 694
   harmful 904
   fearful 355
   hateful *721*
   unsavory 668
shoe *590*

Here is what you would find when you turned to entry #590 to find another word for *shoe*.

590. **CLOTHING.**—*N.* **clothing,** covering, garment, costume, attire, vestment.
   outfit, uniform, suit, gear, equipment.
   dress, suit, evening clothes, tuxedo.
   cloak, cape, mantle, shawl.
   jacket, vest, waistcoat.
   headdress, hat, sombrero, cap, bonnet.
   shoe, slipper, moccasin, sneaker, sandal, galosh, clog, snowshoe, ski, Oxford, patent leather.

I. M. A. Booksnoop

NAME _____

Sailing by Thesaurus

A. A thesaurus will help you sail through your writing assignments by helping you find interesting words. Use the index to find the key word *good*. Find the list of synonyms for *good*. List three synonyms for *good* that you think are interesting.

_____ _____ _____

B. Use your thesaurus to find a word to replace each underlined word in the paragraph below. Write each replacement word and the entry word or key word that helped you find the replacement.

Sailing in Olden Times

The men who volunteered for an (1) ocean trip in the sailing ships of the 1700s really earned their (2) pay. They had to (3) fight the (4) unfriendly wind and weather. The ship might be (5) sunk by a storm of (6) great (7) strength. Often a ship remained (8) motionless for days. As a (9) result, the trip would be (10) lengthened by many days.

Replacement Words   **Entry or Key Words**

1. _____   _____
2. _____   _____
3. _____   _____
4. _____   _____
5. _____   _____
6. _____   _____
7. _____   _____
8. _____   _____
9. _____   _____
10. _____   _____

NAME _____

Find the Rhyme for Us Using a Thesaurus

Use your thesaurus to find synonyms for the words below. Each clue is a word that rhymes with the answer you will find in the thesaurus.

Words	Clues	Synonyms
1. cripple	name	_____
2. hate	restore	_____
3. crash	subside	_____
4. talkative	vivacious	_____
5. conquer	renew	_____
6. favorable	malicious	_____
7. distort	marble	_____
8. strength	bigger	_____
9. evil	minister	_____
10. lie in wait	clerk	_____
11. counterfeit	lamb	_____
12. idea	lotion	_____
13. explore	robe	_____
14. attention	speed	_____
15. search	rest	_____
16. regret	endorse	_____
17. enemy	low	_____
18. lean and lanky	taunt	_____
19. color	do	_____

I. M. A. Booksnoop

NAME _____

The Thesaurus Goes to the Movies

Light, sound, and motion make a movie special. Use your thesaurus to put each word in the box below into the correct category. If your thesaurus has a Synopsis of Categories section in the front, use it.

Light	Sound	Motion
_____	_____	_____
_____	_____	_____
_____	_____	_____
_____	_____	_____
_____	_____	_____
_____	_____	_____
_____	_____	_____
_____	_____	_____
_____	_____	_____
_____	_____	_____
_____	_____	_____
_____	_____	_____

Word Box

acoustics, activity, actuation, budge, dynamic, emanation, flow, fluorescent, flux, gleam, glimmer, glint, glow, illumination, intonation, kinesis, lucence, luminary, luminescence, luminous, luster, mobilization, monotone, motor, movableness, movement, noise, ongoing, pitch, radiance, report, sheen, sonance, sonic, soniferous, stir, timbre, tonality, tonation, tone, tonic, travel

The Thesaurus 57

NAME _____

Thesaurus Test

A. Read the statements below. Write *true* or *false* next to each one.

_____ 1. A thesaurus lists antonyms under every key word.

_____ 2. A thesaurus will help you pronounce a word correctly.

_____ 3. A thesaurus will help you choose a synonym for a word.

_____ 4. All the words in a dictionary are in a thesaurus.

_____ 5. A thesaurus will help you find words to make your writing more interesting.

B. Use your thesaurus. Rewrite the sentences below using a synonym for each underlined word.

1. Isn't a molecule small? _____

2. The house was on a street. _____

3. The sunset was pretty. _____

4. He walked away quickly. _____

C. Use your thesaurus. Write three synonyms for each word below.

1. story _____ _____ _____

2. friend _____ _____ _____

3. old _____ _____ _____

4. said _____ _____ _____

5. want _____ _____ _____

6. hot _____ _____ _____

7. look _____ _____ _____

8. happy _____ _____ _____

I. M. A. Booksnoop

Unit 6

The Atlas

Objective

The students will become familiar with the structure of an atlas and with its values and limitations.

Suggestions for Use

Map-reading skills are not taught in this unit. This unit will make the atlas a friendly book for your students, one they will feel comfortable using because they know where to look to locate information. These activities can be reused when the group progresses to more complete and complex atlases.

Motivational Riddle
Exploring

SUGGESTIONS FOR USE Use this riddle as the conclusion to your introductory lesson. Attach the riddle to the magnifying glass in the Booksnoop poster. Then have your students choose countries and write their own "exploring" riddles for presentation to the class the following day.

RIDDLE
South of the United States, but north of Argentina.
Southeast of Japan, but northeast of Australia.
West of Venezuela, but north of Ecuador and Peru.
South of Panama, and named for a famous explorer of 1492.
Your atlas will reveal my name to you!
   Answer: Colombia

Bulletin Board
Atlas Match

OBJECTIVE The students will use an atlas to match cities with states.

DESCRIPTION Provide the names of cities and states you wish to be matched. The students match each city with its state by placing the city next to the name of its state. This board can be updated easily by changing the matches.

MATERIALS
- tagboard
- construction paper
- pen
- scissors
- pushpins
- hole punch
- compass or circle patterns

PROCEDURE
1. Decide how many matches you have space for on the bulletin board. Make a list of names of cities and states you want the students to match.
2. Cut five large circles from tagboard. Print one letter of the word *ATLAS* on each circle. Arrange the circles in order vertically on the bulletin board and staple them in place.

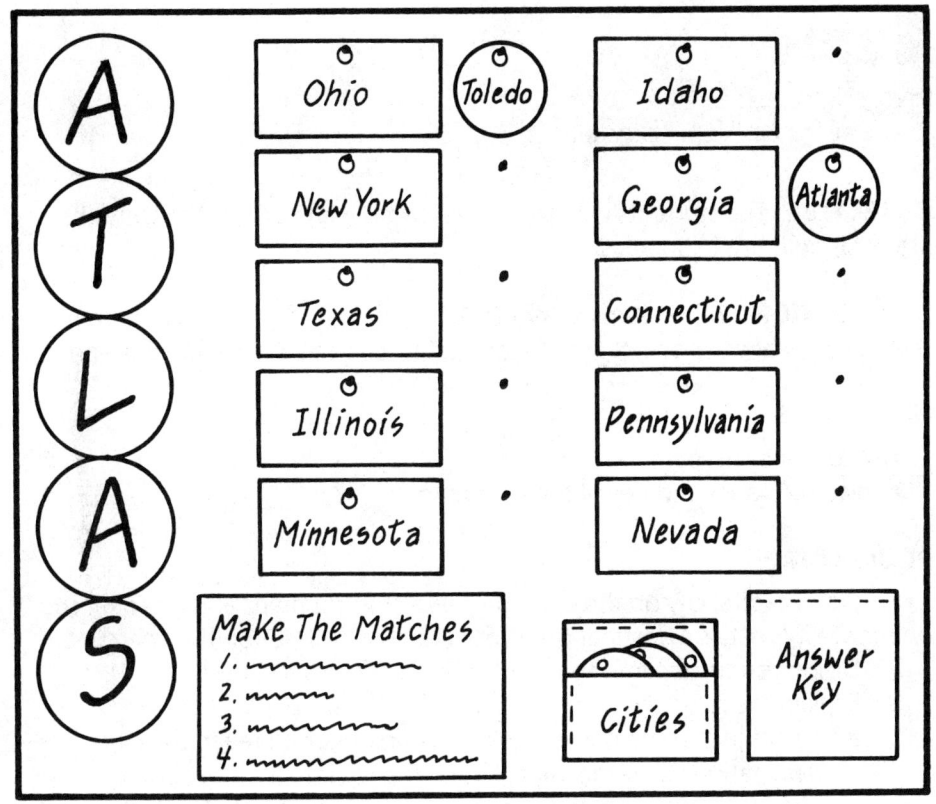

3. Cut a smaller circle from tagboard for each city on your match list. Punch a hole large enough to accommodate the head of a pushpin about 1 inch from the outer edge of each circle. Print a city name on each circle.

4. Cut rectangles from tagboard. Print a state name on each rectangle. Staple the rectangles in position on the bulletin board. Place a pushpin next to each state name.

5. Make a storage pocket by folding a piece of construction paper up one third and stapling along the edges. Label the pocket Cities. Staple the pocket in position on the bulletin board. Place the city name circles in the pocket.

6. Place an atlas at the bulletin board.

7. Print the following directions on a piece of construction paper. Staple it in position on the bulletin board.

Make the Matches
1. Take the circles from the pocket.
2. Match each city with its state by hanging it beside its state.
3. Check your answers by using the atlas index.
4. Return the cities to the pocket when finished.

8. Update this bulletin board by changing the city names.

The Atlas 61

Game
Westward, Ho!

OBJECTIVE The students will trace a westward route across the United States using maps in an atlas.

DESCRIPTION Relay teams compete to be the first to complete a map route through capital cities across the United States to reach a given destination.

MATERIALS
- atlas for each team
- piece of paper and pencil for each team

PROCEDURE
1. Pick a capital city on the east coast as a starting point and a capital city on the west coast as a destination. Write these city names on the chalkboard.
2. Divide your group into teams of three to five players each.
3. Explain the rules:
    a. The object of the game is to be the first team to reach the city of destination using the atlas to plan the route.
    b. The first player uses the atlas to find the location of the starting city. Then the player "travels" to a bordering state and writes the name of its capital city on the game sheet. The game sheet, pencil, and closed atlas is passed to the next player.
    c. The second player finds the state capital listed by the first player, "travels" to a bordering state, and writes the name of its capital city. The game sheet, pencil, and closed atlas are passed to the third player.
    d. The player who reaches the destination writes the city's name, stands up, and says, "Westward, ho!"
    e. When all teams have finished, the routes will be checked for accuracy against a wall map. The first team with a correct route is the winner.

VARIATIONS
1. Increase the level of difficulty by restricting travel to cities of a certain population size.
2. Travel around the world using the capitals of countries.

TRANSPARENCY MASTER

Your Travel Guide: The Atlas

The atlas has two sections that will help you in your travels: the table of contents and the index. Read the examples of these sections below.

Contents

Introduction	1	Resources	
How Maps Are Made	2–4	Mineral	22–23
World Maps		Vegetable	24–25
Physical	5–6	Water Power	26–27
Political	7–8	North America	
Natural Vegetation	9–10	Physical	28
Population	11–12	Land use	29
Soil Groups	13–14	Alaska	30–31
Major Religions	15–16	Canada	32–33

Index

Page	Name	Region	Lat.	Long.
48	John Day R.	Ore.	44 N	120 W
53	John Dayley Nat'l Mon.	S.D.	42 N	103 W
39	Johnson City	N.Y.	42 N	76 W
76	Joinville	Braz.	26 S	48 W
36	Jones C.	Can.	54 N	79 W
101	Jordan	Asia	30 N	38 E
116	Jordan R.	Isr.	31 N	35 E
68	Juan Luis Is.	Cuba	22 N	82 W
96	Juba	Som. (Afr.)	4 N	31 E

I. M. A. Booksnoop reproducible page, copyright © 1983 Pitman Learning, Inc.

NAME _____

Getting Acquainted

Get to know your atlas. Explore the table of contents and any other lists of maps that are in your atlas.

A. Write the number of the page on which you will find each map listed below. There may be more than one page number for a map.

Map	Page
1. Political divisions of the world	_____
2. Physical map of the world	_____
3. Climates of the world	_____
4. Temperatures of the world	_____
5. Rainfall of the world	_____
6. Ocean currents of the world	_____
7. Natural vegetation of the world	_____
8. Soil groups of the world	_____
9. Population of the world	_____
10. Agricultural products of the world	_____
11. Mineral deposits of the world	_____
12. Languages of the world	_____
13. Religions of the world	_____

B. Some atlases have interesting lists—for example, of the world's longest rivers, highest mountains, and largest cities—in the back. Look in the back of your atlas just before the index. Write the names of the other lists you find.

_____

_____

_____

NAME _____

Making Conversation

A. Find the index in your atlas. Locate the entry for each city listed below. Tell the latitude and longitude for each city (if the index lists it) and the page on which you will find it.

City	Lat.	Long.	Page
1. Athens, Greece	_____	_____	_____
2. Bern, Switzerland	_____	_____	_____
3. Cairo, Egypt	_____	_____	_____
4. Toronto, Canada	_____	_____	_____
5. Washington, D.C., U.S.A.	_____	_____	_____
6. Mexico City, Mexico	_____	_____	_____
7. La Paz, Bolivia	_____	_____	_____
8. Sydney, Australia	_____	_____	_____
9. Calcutta, India	_____	_____	_____
10. Seoul, Korea	_____	_____	_____
11. Baghdad, Iraq	_____	_____	_____
12. Mandalay, Burma	_____	_____	_____
13. Ankara, Turkey	_____	_____	_____
14. Caracas, Venezuela	_____	_____	_____
15. Nairobi, Kenya	_____	_____	_____

B. List the names of three other cities that interest you, and complete the table for them.

1. _____ _____ _____ _____

2. _____ _____ _____ _____

3. _____ _____ _____ _____

The Atlas 65

NAME _____

Being Neighborly

Use the table of contents in your atlas to find the maps showing the countries listed below. Write the page number for each one. Turn to the map and find the country's neighbors. Write the names of at least two neighboring countries for each country below.

Country	Page	Neighbors
1. France	_____	_____
2. Sweden	_____	_____
3. Hungary	_____	_____
4. Libya	_____	_____
5. Iraq	_____	_____
6. El Salvador	_____	_____
7. Bolivia	_____	_____
8. India	_____	_____
9. Mexico	_____	_____

I. M. A. Booksnoop

NAME _____

Atlas Test

A. Place a check beside each statement below that is true for your atlas.

___ 1. My atlas has an index of place names.

___ 2. My atlas tells how to pronounce unusual names.

___ 3. My atlas has a table of contents listing the types of maps.

___ 4. My atlas lists the capital cities of the world.

___ 5. My atlas shows the physical features of Mars.

___ 6. My atlas shows the farm products of the world.

___ 7. My atlas helps me spell tricky words.

___ 8. My atlas tells about important explorers.

___ 9. My atlas lists the largest mountains of the world.

___ 10. My atlas lists most of the rivers of the world.

B. Number the entries in each group below in the order in which you would find them in the index of an atlas.

1. ___ New Haven

   ___ N. Park

   ___ Nile River

   ___ Northfield

   ___ New Windsor

2. ___ Lancaster

   ___ L. San Marcos

   ___ Los Altos

   ___ Lincoln

   ___ Le Grand

The Atlas 67

Unit 7

Bartlett's Familiar Quotations

Objective

The students will learn to use *Familiar Quotations,* by John Bartlett.

Before You Begin

Browse through Bartlett's yourself and have some fun finding the origin of the sayings we hear and use every day. If the *Oxford Dictionary of Quotations* is available, compare its contents and structure with Bartlett's. Plan to have your more able students make these comparisons, too.

Motivational Riddle
Meet Mr. Bartlett

SUGGESTIONS FOR USE Use this riddle to introduce your students to Bartlett's *Familiar Quotations*. (The *Oxford Dictionary of Quotations* does not contain the riddle's quotations.) Attach the riddle to the magnifying glass in the Booksnoop poster. After this riddle has been solved, have your students print their favorite quotations to be put on the poster. Have the student who finds the author supply the next quotation.

RIDDLE

Can you tell me who was the one
Who said these words? You'll have fun!
"Little strokes fell great oaks."
Here's another clue, folks:
"An empty bag cannot stand upright."
With these clues, whom do you cite?
One more clue, then I'll cease.
Who said, "There never was a good war or a bad peace"?
   Answer: Benjamin Franklin

Bulletin Board
Match the Pears

OBJECTIVE The students will use *Familiar Quotations* to match quotations with authors.

DESCRIPTION Quotations are written on sentence strips, and the authors' names are printed on pears. The students use *Familiar Quotations* to make the matches.

MATERIALS
- five sheets of yellow tagboard
- sentence strips
- pen
- stapler
- pushpins
- hole punch

PROCEDURE

   1. Choose the quotations you wish to use. Print each quotation on a sentence strip. Write the author's name on the back for your reference.
   2. Cut two large pears from yellow tagboard and print MATCH THE on one and USE BARTLETT'S on the other. Staple them in position on the bulletin board.

Bartlett's Familiar Quotations 69

3. Cut out smaller pears. You will need a small pear for each quotation and two more to complete the caption. Position the two caption pears next to the MATCH THE pear and staple it to the board.

4. Print an author's name on each of the remaining pears. Punch a hole in the stem end of each pear. The hole must be large enough to allow the pear to be suspended from a pushpin.

5. Arrange the sentence strips as shown in the illustration. Place a pushpin at the end of each sentence strip.

6. Print an answer key and staple it to the bulletin board. Cover the key with a piece of paper stapled at the top to make a flap. Label it Answer Key.

7. Make a storage pocket for the author pears by folding up the bottom third of a piece of paper and stapling the edges. Staple the pocket to the bulletin board.

8. Print the following directions on a piece of paper and staple it to the bulletin board.

Match the Pears

1. Read the quotations.
2. Take the author's name pears from the pocket.
3. Use Bartlett's to find the author of each quotation.
4. Hang the author's name beside his or her quote.
5. Check the answer key and return the pears to the pocket when finished.

Game
Bart-ades

OBJECTIVE The students will use Bartlett's to find quotations.

DESCRIPTION Adapt the familiar game of Charades to provide an enjoyable break for your students. Allow time for the students to find quotations to contribute to the game.

MATERIALS
- Bartlett's *Familiar Quotations*
- slip of paper and pen for each player
- shoe box

PROCEDURE

1. Plan ahead for this game. Several days in advance, have each participant find a quotation in Bartlett's that can be pantomimed. Direct them to copy the quotation and its author's name on a slip of paper and place it in the box.
2. On the day of the game, explain the rules:
   a. The object of the game is to be the first to say the quotation correctly.
   b. The first player begins the game by drawing a slip from the box.
   c. The player reads the slip silently, announces its author, and then pantomimes the quote.
   d. The other players will guess the words as they are pantomimed.
   e. When all the words have been pantomimed, the player calls on students to say the entire quotation.
   f. The first student to say it correctly draws the next slip.
   g. The player who contributed the quotation watches as the group plays.

VARIATION

Play Bart-ades in teams. Each team prepares a list of quotations for the other team to pantomime and guess.

TRANSPARENCY MASTER

Meet Mr. Bartlett

Below is part of an index of the type used by Mr. Bartlett in compiling his book.

Happy and sad, 672
    as a clam, 325
    as kings, 478
    as the grass was green, 905
    consider, and the, 342
    goes as lucky goes, 660
    never so, as we suppose, 512
    the man whose wish, 596

Below is an example of an entry in Bartlett's *Familiar Quotations*.

ARTHUR GUITERMAN
(1871–1943)

Oh, the saddest of sights in a world of sin
Is a little lost pup with his tail tucked in!
    Little Lost Pup, Stanza 1

He stood with his muzzle thrust out through the door
The whole forty days of that terrible pour!
Because of which drenching, the Sages unfold,
The Nose of a Healthy Dog always is Cold.[1]
    The Dog's Cold Nose

[1] Most frozen was his honest nose,
And never could it lose again
The dampness of that dreadful rain.
    MARGARET EYTINGE,
    Why the Dog's Nose Is Cold

72 I. M. A. Booksnoop

NAME _____

Getting in Step with Bartlett

Bartlett's has two indexes: an index of authors and an index of quotations. All entries are alphabetical. To find a quotation, you need to find its key word first. The key words of some quotations are listed below, along with their key lines. Number each group of key lines in the order in which they would appear in the index.

1. fields

___ babbled of green

___ of air

___ and the gliding streams

___ boundless and beautiful

___ and the waters shout

2. cat

___ so sweet a

___ bell the

___ nine lives like a

___ feet, fog comes on little

___ in the pan

3. city

___ is greater than its bricks

___ in the sea

___ is historic

___ is the teacher of man

___ is not builded in a day

4. friend

___ in need

___ dog is man's best

___ faithful is the best

___ equal to a brother

___ who deserts you

I. M. A. Booksnoop reproducible page, copyright © 1983 Pitman Learning, Inc.

Bartlett's Familiar Quotations 73

NAME _____

Who Said That?

Read each quotation below. Circle the key word that will help you find each quotation in the index of lines in Bartlett's. Then find each quotation and write the name of the person who said it.

1. All that we see or seem

   Is but a dream within a dream. _____

2. An' the Gobble-uns 'at gits you

       Ef you

           Don't

               Watch

                   Out! _____

3. It is not only fine feathers that make fine birds.

   _____

4. Time is but the stream I go a-fishing in. _____

5. As idle as a painted ship

   Upon a painted ocean. _____

6. In love of home, the love of country has its rise.

   _____

7. To be great is to be misunderstood. _____

8. A sharp tongue is the only edge tool that grows keener with

   constant use. _____

9. I think that I shall never see

   A poem lovely as a tree. _____

10. I think that I shall never see

    A billboard lovely as a tree.

    Indeed, unless the billboards fall,

    I'll never see a tree at all. _____

74 I. M. A. Booksnoop

NAME _____

The Case of the Interrupted Quotation

Someone has been playing tricks with your tape recorder! Use Bartlett's to find the missing line or lines of each quotation below. Circle the key word that will help you find each line in the index. Then find the quotation and complete the sentence or stanza.

1. One if by land, _____

2. Fifteen men on the Dead Man's Chest— _____

3. Tiger! tiger! burning bright _____

4. Has thou named all the birds without a gun? _____

5. To err is human, _____

6. O Captain! my Captain! _____

Bartlett's Familiar Quotations 75

NAME _____

Bartlett's Test

A. Read each sentence below. Write *true* or *false* next to each one.

_____ 1. Bartlett's index is arranged alphabetically by key words from the quotations.

_____ 2. All the writings or sayings of a famous person are recorded in Bartlett's.

_____ 3. There is a table of contents in Bartlett's.

_____ 4. Only Americans are quoted in Bartlett's.

_____ 5. Bartlett's lists only quotations that are less than 100 years old.

B. Circle the key word or words that would help you find each quotation below.

1. They also serve who only stand and wait.
2. Some books are to be tasted, others to be swallowed, and some few to be chewed and digested.
3. For fools rush in where angels fear to tread.
4. Happy is the house that shelters a friend.
5. Three may keep a secret, if two of them are dead.
6. The reward of a thing well done, is to have done it.
7. Rose is a rose is a rose is a rose.
8. Something there is that doesn't love a wall.
9. It's all in the day's work.
10. If wishes were horses, beggars might ride.

76 I. M. A. Booksnoop

Unit 8

The Almanac

Objective

The students will become familiar with the almanac and the many types of information it presents.

Before You Begin

Gather as many almanacs as you can. Almanacs do not have to be up-to-date to provide the type of practice the students need to learn to use an almanac.

Motivational Riddle
Department Store for Questioners

SUGGESTIONS FOR USE Use this riddle to encourage your students to dig into the almanac. Fill in the blanks in the riddle to correspond to the facts you choose from your almanacs. Attach the riddle to the magnifying glass in the Booksnoop poster. After the riddle has been solved, have your students find their own facts. Substitute the students' questions for lines five through eight.

RIDDLE

The almanac is a great book to read!
In it are facts to fill every need.
Here are some questions, the answers to which
You'll find in the almanac—it's a cinch!
In 19____ what male actor won the Oscar?
In the Olympic shot put, who was the star?
From _____ to _____ is how many miles?
How many tornadoes in the weather files?
You'll find all those answers and many more,
In the almanac, the book department store!
   Answer: Use your almanac to determine the correct answers.

Bulletin Board
Elapsed Events

OBJECTIVE The students will use the almanac to find events that occurred on given dates.

DESCRIPTION The students will complete the bulletin board by finding events that match the dates of the calendar you prepare. The almanac search that results will familiarize your students with the myriad information available in an almanac.

MATERIALS
- bulletin board backing paper, approximately 2 feet by 3 feet
- construction paper
- pen
- meter stick
- stapler
- almanacs

BOOKSNOOP'S ELAPSED EVENTS MONTH

PROCEDURE

1. Prepare a calendar grid for a month of your choice on backing paper. Number the days in the top left corners of the grid spaces. Staple the grid to the bulletin board.

2. Use the overhead projection method to reproduce the picture of I. M. A. Booksnoop (see page 1). Staple the picture to the bulletin board.

3. Prepare the caption by printing the bulletin board title on pieces of construction paper. Staple the title to the bulletin board.

4. Cut rectangular pieces of construction paper for the students' answers. Size them to fit the grid spaces while allowing the date to show.

5. Have each student select a date to research. When an event is found for that date, print the item on a rectangle and staple it in place on the calendar.

The Almanac 79

Game
Categories—Nobel Awards

OBJECTIVE The students will use an almanac to find the names of Nobel Award winners.

DESCRIPTION Teams or individuals compete to fill in the most names on a grid.

MATERIALS
- ditto master for game sheet
- pencil for each player or team
- almanac for each player or team

PROCEDURE
1. Prepare a ditto master of the categories game sheet.

NOBEL	A	W	A	R	D	S
Physics						
Chemistry						
Peace						
Literature						

  2. Choose team or individual play and prepare the number of copies of the game sheet accordingly.

  3. Explain the rules to the players:
    a. The object of the game is to earn the most points by finding the most names to fill in the grid.
    b. Use the almanac as your reference.
    c. Each name must fit a category and must begin with a letter at the top of a column.
    d. The time limit will be _____ .
    e. When the time is up, one point is awarded for each correct name. The highest score wins.

TRANSPARENCY MASTER

Using the Fact Locator

Here is a portion of a typical almanac index.

Radio
   actors, actresses 356
   awards 357
   inventions 765
   stations, U.S. 931
Red Cross 154
Reno, Nevada 456–457
   buildings 488
   mayor 320
   population 124,679
Rivers
   dams 712–713

   freight 592
   United States 434
   longest 687
   world 688–689
Roosevelt, Franklin D. . . 264
   birthday 837
   Congress sessions 901
   death 586
   N.R.A. 918
   wife, family 420
Ross, Betsy 259

A. Use the index above. Tell the page number on which you might find each of the facts below. (You may not be able to find them all.)

_____ 1. What is the world's longest river?

_____ 2. Did President Roosevelt have children?

_____ 3. Is Johnny Carson a radio actor?

_____ 4. What is the tallest building in Reno, Nevada?

_____ 5. How many major dams are there in California?

_____ 6. How much rye did Canada produce last year?

_____ 7. Which U.S. river has the most tributaries?

_____ 8. When was Betsy Ross born?

B. Use the index above to name the subtopic that would help you answer each question below.

_____ 1. How many tons of freight were shipped on the Mississippi River last year?

_____ 2. Is the Colorado River longer than the Missouri River?

_____ 3. Who invented the radio?

_____ 4. How many people live in Reno, Nevada?

NAME _____

Which Department?

A. The almanac will give you up-to-date information. Use it when you want the most recent facts. Read the list of research questions below. Write *yes* if the almanac would be the best reference book because you need up-to-date facts. If another type of reference book would be more helpful, name the type of book you would use.

_____yes_____ a. Who won the college basketball championship last year?

encyclopedia b. Did George Washington write the Constitution of the United States?

_____ 1. Who is the governor of Texas?

_____ 2. How many square miles are there in the state of Ohio?

_____ 3. When will be the next eclipse of the sun?

_____ 4. When did William Penn begin the colony of Pennsylvania?

_____ 5. Who holds the record for the most hours of space travel?

_____ 6. What is the population of New York City?

_____ 7. How is steel made?

_____ 8. How much steel did Japan produce last year?

B. Now you are ready to find the "departments" in the big "store" of facts called the almanac. The key to this store is the index, which is usually found in the *front* of the almanac. There may also be a short index in the back. Use the index of an almanac to find the entry for your state. Name five subtopics listed for your state.

_____

_____

_____

I. M. A. Booksnoop

NAME _____

Department, Please!

A. In a large department store like the almanac, you need to know which "section," or index topic, will help you find the fact you want. Write which topic you would look for in the index to help answer each question below.

___football___   a. How many touchdowns did O. J. Simpson score?

___presidents___   b. When did Thomas Jefferson serve as the President of the United States?

_____ 1. How many home runs did Hank Aaron hit?

_____ 2. How many weather satellites are still operating?

_____ 3. Who invented touch-tone dialing?

_____ 4. How many automobiles were sold in the United States last year?

_____ 5. Who is the president of the United Nations?

_____ 6. What products does the Republic of South Africa produce besides gold?

_____ 7. Which place in the United States had the coldest temperature last year?

_____ 8. Which country produced the most coffee last year?

_____ 9. What is the current automobile speed record and who holds it?

_____ 10. How many moons does Saturn have?

B. Use the almanac to find the answers to five of the questions listed above. Write the number of each question and the answer.

_____

_____

_____

_____

The Almanac 83

NAME _____

Only the Facts, Please!

Detectives have to know how to ask questions. Use the index in your almanac to find the page numbers for each main entry listed below. Read the information about each entry and write an interesting question about it. Write the answer, too.

1. Animals: pages _____ to _____

Question: _____

Answer: _____

2. Inventions: pages _____ to _____

Question: _____

Answer: _____

3. Trees: pages _____ to _____

Question: _____

Answer: _____

4. Volcanoes: pages _____ to _____

Question: _____

Answer: _____

5. Weather — Record Temperatures: pages _____ to _____

Question: _____

Answer: _____

6. Tornadoes: pages _____ to _____

Question: _____

Answer: _____

I. M. A. Booksnoop

NAME _____

Almanac Test

A. For each question below, write *yes* if the almanac would be the best reference book to use to answer the question. Write *no* if another reference book would be more helpful.

_____ 1. Who holds the record for the mile run?

_____ 2. How are laser rays controlled?

_____ 3. How did Alabama get its name?

_____ 4. What are some of Benjamin Franklin's famous sayings?

_____ 5. Is the Nile River longer than the Amazon River?

_____ 6. Who holds the record for the longest punt?

_____ 7. Did George Washington visit France while he was president?

_____ 8. Who wrote *A Midsummer Night's Dream*?

_____ 9. How many kings of England have been named Henry?

_____ 10. How many people live in Washington, D.C.?

B. Write which main topic you would look for to help you answer each question below.

_____ 1. What is the world's biggest animal?

_____ 2. How many barrels of oil did the United States import last year?

_____ 3. Did Abraham Lincoln have any brothers and sisters?

_____ 4. What is the largest lake in Minnesota?

_____ 5. Who holds the track record for the Indianapolis 500?

Unit 9

The Encyclopedia

Objective

The students will become familiar with the scope and limitations of an encyclopedia and will locate specific information in available encyclopedias.

Before You Begin

Alphabetizing and index skills allow easy access to the information in an encyclopedia. Use the activities in units 1 and 2 to refine your students' skills in these areas. Note taking rather than verbatim copying should be stressed as you present the second and fourth activities in this unit.

Motivational Riddle
Can You Find It?

SUGGESTIONS FOR USE Use this riddle as the conclusion to your introduction of the encyclopedia. Attach the riddle to the magnifying glass in the Booksnoop poster. Have your students make pairs of rhyming questions to replace lines seven and eight of the riddle.

RIDDLE
For Garfield, glaciers, and gold, look in G.
Tolstoy and Texas you will find in T.
For facts about everything—from armadilloes to Morse—
Your encyclopedia is just the source.
Here are a few questions made to puzzle you.
Let's give it a try to see what you can do.
Who in the world made the first printing press?
What creature supposedly lives in Loch Ness?
When was the start of the French Revolution?
In your encyclopedia you'll find each solution.
   Answers: Johann Gutenberg; the Loch Ness monster; 1789

Bulletin Board
I'm in a Pickle!

OBJECTIVE The students will use the encyclopedia to answer questions.

DESCRIPTION The students get out of a "pickle" by finding the answers to teacher-prepared questions. The questions and answers are written on pickles.

MATERIALS
- green and brown construction paper
- black felt-tip pen
- scissors
- small box, at least six inches long
- stapler
- encyclopedia

PROCEDURE

1. Prepare a list of questions. You will need at least one question for each student. We found the almanac to be a great source of question ideas.

2. Make the caption. Cut out I'M IN A from construction paper. Cut out a large green pickle and print PICKLE on it. Staple these to the bulletin board.

The Encyclopedia 87

3. Cut the pickle barrel from brown construction paper. Use a black felt-tip pen to highlight the barrel and label it Pickle Barrel. Staple the barrel in position on the bulletin board.

4. Cover the small box with brown construction paper. Staple one side of the box to the top of the pickle barrel. Label the box Pickle Questions.

5. Prepare the question and answer pickles on green construction paper. You will need a small pickle and a large pickle for each question. Make extra pickles if you want this bulletin board to be an on-going activity. Cut out the pickles and print a question on each small pickle. Put the question pickles in the pickle barrel box.

6. Present the bulletin board to your students. Have each student choose a question pickle and answer the question. Give them large pickles on which to write their answers. Then staple each question pickle beside its answer pickle on the bulletin board. Soon the bulletin board will be covered with information gained from the encyclopedia.

7. When all of your questions have been answered, challenge your students to prepare their own question pickles.

Games

Verify the Facts

OBJECTIVE The students will use encyclopedias to verify statements.

DESCRIPTION Teams compete to be the first to verify a given list of facts. Finding entries quickly and skimming material are the skills enhanced by this game.

MATERIALS
- ditto masters
- sets of encyclopedias
- pencil and game sheet for each team

PROCEDURE

1. Before the day of the game, divide your students into teams of four or five players each. Assign a set of encyclopedias or a portion of a set to each team.

2. Prepare a list of statements, some true, some false, for each team to verify. (See the sample below.) Make the difficulty and number of statements commensurate with the abilities of your students. Each statement must be verifiable in the set (or portion of the set) of encyclopedias assigned to that team. For example, if team 1 is assigned volumes A–L, their game sheet statements must contain information found in volumes A–L.

3. Put the game sheets on ditto masters so that you can use this game with other groups.

4. On the day of the game, assign the students to their teams and encyclopedias.

5. Explain the rules:
   a. The object of the game is to score the most points.
   b. Each team will be given a list of statements that can be verified in the encyclopedias given to the team.
   c. Choose a recorder for your team.
   d. Read all the statements and decide if each is true or false. The recorder writes *true* or *false* to show the team opinion. These cannot be changed.
   e. The team consults the encyclopedias to find the facts that verify the statements. The recorder writes the facts as they are located.

The Encyclopedia 89

f. The scoring is one point for each correct true or false, five points for each correct fact, and a bonus of one point for each correct fact to the team that finishes first.

6. Variation (teacher timesaver): Have the predetermined teams prepare the game sheets.

SAMPLE GAME SHEET ITEM

1. Statement: According to Greek mythology, Pegasus was a flying horse.

Team opinion: _____

Encyclopedia: Volume _____ Page _____

Fact: _____

_____

Encyclopedia Categories

OBJECTIVE The students will use the encyclopedia to locate entries that fit given categories.

PROCEDURE

1. See the almanac version of this game, page 80, for the basic setup. Then adjust it as follows.
2. Make teams of five players each.
3. Use volumes of the encyclopedia as the headings of the columns.
4. Use Country, Person, Element, Animal, and Invention as the categories.
5. Change rule c to: "Each item must fit a category, must begin with a letter at the top of a column, and must be an entry in your encyclopedia."

TRANSPARENCY MASTER

Finding the Keys

A. An encyclopedia detective needs keys—key words that is! What is the key word you would look under to find the answer to each question below?

_____ 1. What is the difference between an aneroid barometer and a mercury barometer?

_____ 2. Where was the civilization of the Incas located?

_____ 3. How is gasoline made?

_____ 4. When did the dodo become extinct?

_____ 5. How does a helicopter fly?

_____ 6. What training did a knight receive?

_____ 7. Where do plastics come from?

_____ 8. What is the speed of light?

_____ 9. How do you tie a bowline knot?

_____ 10. What is natural immunity?

B. Sometimes you will need to use cross-references and the encyclopedia's index. Match each key word below with a cross-reference.

Key Word　　　　　　　　　**Cross-reference**

___ 1. Comets　　　　　　　a. *see also* Textiles

___ 2. Nervous system　　　b. *see also* Solar system

___ 3. Robins　　　　　　　　c. *see also* Human body

___ 4. Water cycle　　　　　d. *see also* Birds

___ 5. Linen　　　　　　　　e. *see also* Weather

The Encyclopedia 91

NAME _____

Using the Keys

A. Before you unlock your encyclopedia, check the copyright date. What does the copyright date tell you about the information in the encyclopedia? _____
_____

B. Now you will have to use your set of encyclopedias. Write the name of your set. _____

Choose one of the following topics to research. Circle your choice.

albatrosses	jellyfish	submarines
bananas	kangaroos	tin
crocodiles	lions	unicorns
diamonds	mastodons	volcanoes
ermines	nickel	whales
flags	orangutans	xenon
grasshoppers	platypuses	yaks
heraldry	Quebec	zodiac
Iceland	radio	

C. Locate your topic in the encyclopedia and read the information. Look for five important facts. Write these facts in phrases below. (A good note-taker does not need to copy complete sentences.)

1. _____
2. _____
3. _____
4. _____
5. _____

D. Write your notes in paragraph form on another piece of paper.

NAME _____

Who Did It?

A. When you are looking for information about a person, you must use the last name to locate the entry. If a person is royalty and does not use a last name, you would look under the first name; for example, to find Queen Elizabeth II, you would look under *Elizabeth*. Write the letter of the volume you would use to locate each name below.

___ 1. Harry S. Truman   ___ 4. Amelia Earhart

___ 2. King George III   ___ 5. Eli Whitney

___ 3. Anton Dvorak   ___ 6. Lady Jane Grey

B. Now you are ready to use your encyclopedia to find out "who did it." Below is a list of inventions. Find out who invented each one. Write the volume and the page number where you found the answer, and write the name of the inventor. (There may be more than one name.)

Invention	Vol.	Page	Inventor(s)
1. Adding machine			
2. Air conditioning			
3. Electric battery			
4. Elevator			
5. Cash register			
6. Dynamite			
7. Gasoline engine			
8. Geiger counter			
9. Modern bicycle			
10. Kaleidoscope			
11. Motorcycle			
12. Oleomargarine			
13. Parachute			

The Encyclopedia

NAME _____

Discover the Details

A detective must know a lot about the world. Read the projects below. Each can be researched in an encyclopedia. Choose a project to research. (This is the hardest part. Choose carefully and stick to your choice.)

1. How are coded messages cracked? Make some coded messages using famous codes. Prepare them in chart form.

2. How did our system for telling time develop? Take notes and then prepare an oral or written report. Show the world time zones on a map.

3. Was our calendar always the way it is now? List the changes that have taken place. Make a chart showing how the months got their names.

4. The world of stars is endless. Find out how stars are classified by scientists and write the information in chart form. Make diagrams of at least five constellations.

5. Find out about rocks. Learn the names of the rocks found in your area. Make a rock collection and label your findings.

6. Find out about trees. Learn the names of the trees found in your area. Make a leaf collection and label each leaf. Draw a cross section of a typical tree trunk. Label the parts.

7. How many bones are in the human body? Make a diagram of the human skeleton and label the largest bones. Write a report explaining different types of bone fractures.

8. How are weather predictions made? Prepare an oral or written report about instruments that meteorologists use to predict weather. Include diagrams.

9. Where did our number system originate? Make charts of other number systems. Write a paragraph summarizing the history of our decimal system.

10. Did you ever wonder how a ship knows where it is going in the middle of the ocean? Prepare an oral or written report about navigation. Try to find a navigator's chart to include with your report.

I. M. A. Booksnoop

NAME _____

Discover the Details *continued*

11. What is a laser? How does it work? How are they useful to us? Prepare an oral or written report to answer these questions. Include diagrams.

12. How have clothing styles changed in the last 200 years? List the periods of clothing styles. Illustrate your information.

13. Oil is an important natural resource. How was oil formed? How is oil changed into gasoline? Prepare an oral or written report. Include diagrams.

14. Choose a president of the United States who is not well known. Write a biographical sketch about him.

15. Write a biographical sketch about one of these famous women: Elizabeth C. Stanton, Marie Curie, Florence Nightingale, Harriet Tubman, Maria Mitchell, Harriet Beecher Stowe, Susan B. Anthony, or Elizabeth I.

16. How does a gasoline engine work? Prepare a diagram of an engine. Write an explanation of each main part. Explain the difference between diesel engines and gasoline engines.

17. Research the history of flight. Make a time line of the main events. Be sure to include enough information to make your time line informative. Add illustrations for more interest.

18. Investigate the history of your favorite sport. Prepare an oral or written report. Include diagrams if possible.

19. Research the steps in preparing a typical television show from script development to broadcast. Present your information in a flowchart if you know how, or present your facts in a cartoon or a written report.

20. Choose your own topic for research. List the things you wish to find out and have your teacher approve it first.

The Encyclopedia

NAME _____

Encyclopedia Test

A. Read each statement. Then write *true* or *false* in the blank.

_____ 1. An encyclopedia never has an index.

_____ 2. You should check the copyright date of an encyclopedia before you use the information.

_____ 3. Entries in an encyclopedia are arranged by age, from oldest to newest.

_____ 4. There may be more than one place in the encyclopedia that has information about your topic.

_____ 5. People are listed by their last names in an encyclopedia.

B. Circle the key word or words in each question below that would help you find the encyclopedia entry to answer the question. Then write the letter of the volume you would use in the blank.

___ 1. What are the phases of the moon?

___ 2. What is the number of known elements?

___ 3. How is the length of a calendar year determined?

___ 4. Who introduced the use of antiseptics?

___ 5. Which explorer discovered Alaska?

___ 6. How do plants take in water and food?

___ 7. When was the French and Indian War?

___ 8. What causes an eclipse?

___ 9. Why was Marco Polo important?

___ 10. Why do we remember King Henry VIII?

Unit 10

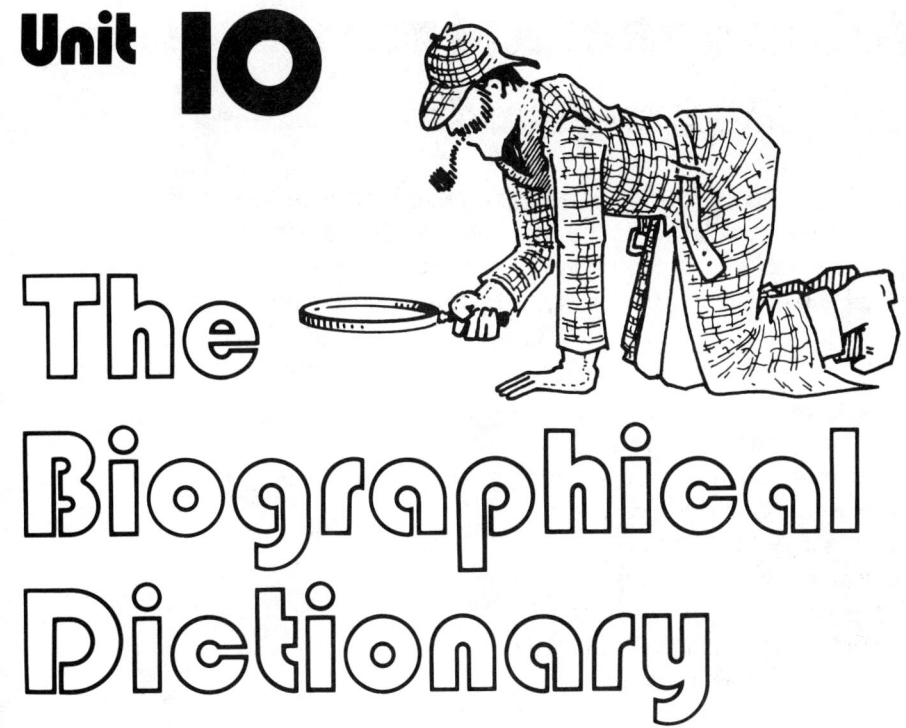

The Biographical Dictionary

Objective

The students will become familiar with the contents, use, and limitations of a biographical dictionary.

Before You Begin

All of the activities in this unit require the use of *Webster's Biographical Dictionary*. Since most schools usually have a limited number of copies of this book, we suggest you use the worksheets as learning centers. To be sure all students are exposed to the biographical dictionary, use the bulletin board, World's Most Wanted Wonderful Winners, pages 98–99. Obtain copies of the other types of biographical dictionaries and make them available to your group, too.

Motivational Riddle
He Spread Light

SUGGESTIONS FOR USE Use this riddle to introduce your students to the biographical dictionary as a time saver. Attach the riddle to the magnifying glass in the Booksnoop poster. When a few basic facts about a person are required, a biographical dictionary is the reference of preference!

RIDDLE
In my last, my first is E.
My second is the fourth, you'll see.
Through my third, my fourth—a snake—is seen.
My fifth is round and not very lean.
My sixth is in not but not in dot.
Look me over, what have you got?
An American man, you might say,
Who spread his light in a special way!
   Answer: Thomas A. Edison

Bulletin Board
World's Most Wanted Wonderful Winners

OBJECTIVE The students will use the biographical dictionary to match famous people with their descriptions.

DESCRIPTION Stars and pictures of famous people highlight this bulletin board. Short biographies are written on cards, and the students use the biographical dictionary to make matches.

SUGGESTIONS FOR USE Use this bulletin board to introduce the biographical dictionary to your group. Then have your students find pictures of famous people and write the matching biographies.

MATERIALS
- biographical dictionary
- yellow construction paper
- scissors
- tagboard
- pushpins
- hole punch
- pictures of famous people

PROCEDURE

1. Choose pictures of people who are listed in the biographical dictionary. The number you choose will depend on the area of your bulletin board.

2. Cut out a star from yellow construction paper for each picture. Staple the stars to the bulletin board.

3. Mount each picture on tagboard. Number the tagboard and write the person's name on it. Fasten each picture on or beside a star. Place a pushpin at the bottom of each picture.

4. Prepare the biography cards. Cut squares of tagboard that go well with the size of your stars. Punch a hole in each card about 1 inch from the top.

5. Write a biographical facts card for each picture. Include a few nonmatches if you wish. Assign a letter to each card.

6. Place several pushpins near the bottom of the bulletin board and hang the facts cards on them.

7. Prepare the caption and staple it to the bulletin board.

8. Write the challenge rhyme on a piece of construction paper and staple it to the bulletin board. The rhyme is:

What did these talented persons do?
The biographical dictionary will give you a clue.
Look up the facts, and pick the right card.
Hang it under the picture — that's not hard!
Check your answers and put the cards back when you're through.

9. Make an answer key, cover it with a flap, and staple it to the bulletin board.

The Biographical Dictionary 99

Game
Unscramble

OBJECTIVE The students will unscramble a set of letters to find a famous person's last name and use the biographical dictionary to find the first name.

DESCRIPTION A teacher-prepared game sheet challenges the students to discover the hidden names. Biographical clues are given. Then the biographical dictionary is checked to find the first names.

SUGGESTIONS FOR USE This game lends itself to team or individual play. Make it an individual activity if your supply of biographical dictionaries is limited. The frustration level may be too high for less able students.

MATERIALS
- game sheet and pencil for each player or team
- biographical dictionary for each player or team

PROCEDURE

1. Decide if you wish to make Unscramble a team game or an individual activity. Reproduce the appropriate number of game sheets. You will need a sheet for each individual or a sheet for each team.

2. For team play, explain the rules:
   a. The object of the game is to be the first team to unscramble all the famous persons' last names and find their first names in the biographical dictionary.
   b. Each team will be given a dictionary, a game sheet, and a pencil. When the signal is given, begin unscrambling.
   c. When all teams are finished, the team with the most correct answers is the winner.

SAMPLE GAMESHEET: UNSCRAMBLE

Directions: Unscramble the last names in column 2. Use the biographical dictionary to find the first names and write them in column 3. The clues in column 4 will help you. Write the first letter of each last name in column 1. The correct letters will spell the last name of another famous person.

1	2	3	4
___	staeanm	_____, _____	Kodak camera man
___	nivgir	_____, _____	Author
___	dansgrbu	_____, _____	Poet
___	rahtare	_____, _____	Aviator
___	sant	_____, _____	Cartoonist
___	yeash	_____, _____	U.S. president
___	soit	_____, _____	Elevator man
___	swihlert	_____, _____	Artist
___	stnieien	_____, _____	Physicist
___	veerer	_____, _____	American patriot

ANSWERS: Eastman, George; **I**rving, Washington; **S**andburg, Carl; **E**arhart, Amelia; **N**ast, Thomas; **H**ayes, Rutherford B.; **O**tis, Elisha; **W**histler, James A. M.; **E**instein, Albert; **R**evere, Paul

The Biographical Dictionary 101

Biographical Dictionary Page

Jeffers 777 **Jelačić od Bužima**

Jef'fers (jĕf'ērz), **Robinson**, *in full* John Robinson. 1887–1962. American poet, b. Pittsburgh, Pa. Author of *Californians* (1916), *Tamar* (1924), *Cawdor* (1928), *Dear Judas* (1929), *Thurso's Landing* (1932), *Solstice* (1935), *Such Counsels You Gave to Me* (1937), etc.

Jeffers, William Martin. 1876–1953. American railway official, b. North Platte, Nebr.; rose from office boy (1890) to president (1937–46) of Union Pacific R.R.; U.S. rubber administrator (1942–43).

Jef'fer·son (jĕf'ēr·s'n), **Charles Edward**. 1860–1937. American Congregational clergyman; pastor of Broadway Tabernacle, New York City (1898–1937).

Jefferson, Joseph. 1829–1905. American actor, b. Philadelphia; made success in Laura Keene's company, New York, as Asa Trenchard in *Our American Cousin* (1858), and Caleb Plummer in *The Cricket on the Hearth* (1859). Most famous role, Rip Van Winkle in Dion Boucicault's play of that name (from 1865). Also made success of Bob Acres in *The Rivals* (from 1880). His grandfather **Joseph Jefferson** (1774–1832), b. Plymouth, Eng., came to U.S. (1795) and appeared chiefly in comedy roles. See also Eleanor FARJEON.

Jefferson, Thomas. 1743–1826. Third president of the United States, b. in Goochland, now Albemarle County, Va. Grad. William and Mary (1762). Adm. to bar (1767). Member, Virginia House of Burgesses (1769–74); with R. H. Lee and Patrick Henry initiated intercolonial committee of correspondence (1773). Member, Continental Congress (1775, 1776); chairman of committee that prepared Declaration of Independence; wrote and presented first draft of declaration to Congress (July 2, 1776); signed Declaration of Independence. Governor of Virginia (1779–81). Again member, Continental Congress (1783–85). U.S. minister to France (1785–89). U.S. secretary of state (1790–93); differing policies caused bitter antagonism with Alexander Hamilton, secretary of treasury. Vice-president of the U.S. (1797–1801); president of the U.S. (1801–09), elected by House of Representatives after tie in popular vote (with Aaron Burr, *q.v.*). Features of administration: purchase of Louisiana, war against Algerian pirates, westward expansion, diplomatic trouble with Great Britain over impressment of American seamen (Embargo Act of 1807), prohibition of the importation of slaves. On retirement from presidency, lived on plantation near "Monticello," near Charlottesville, Va. Instrumental in founding U. of Virginia (1819). Elected to American Hall of Fame (1900).

Jef'frey (jĕf'rĭ), **Francis**. Lord **Jeffrey**. 1773–1850. Scottish critic and jurist, b. in Edinburgh. One of founders of *Edinburgh Review* (1802), and its editor (1803–29). Judge of Court of Session (1834–50). Author of the famous devastating criticism of Wordsworth's *Excursion* beginning "This will never do."

Jef'freys (jĕf'rĭz), **George**. 1st Baron **Jeffreys of Wem** (wĕm). 1644–1689. English jurist. Solicitor general to duke of York (1677). Lord chief justice (1682) and privy councilor (1683); lord chancellor (1685). On overthrow of James II, attempted to flee from England but was captured and imprisoned in Tower of London (1688), where he died (April 18, 1689). As chief justice and chancellor, made himself notorious by injustice and brutality. The assizes conducted by him (1685) at which those involved in Monmouth's rebellion against James II were tried became known as the Bloody Assizes because of the number of executions decreed.

Jef'fries (jĕf'rĭz), **James J.** 1875–1953. American prizefighter; world heavyweight champion from 1899 (winning title from Bob Fitzsimmons) until he retired in 1905; returned to ring for match with Jack Johnson (1910), in which he was defeated.

Jeffries, John. 1744–1819. Physician and balloonist, b. Boston; practiced medicine in Boston. Loyalist during American Revolution; resident in England after the war. Interested himself in use of balloons for scientific observations and experiments; with François Blanchard, French aeronaut, crossed English Channel from Dover to forest of Guînes, France, in balloon (Jan. 7, 1785), first crossing of English Channel by air.

Jehan. See SHAH JAHAN.

Jehangir. See JAHANGIR.

Je·ho'a·haz (jē·hō'à·hăz). See AHAZ.

Jehoahaz. In Douay Bible **Jo'a·chaz** (jō'à·kăz). (1) King of Israel (d. 800? B.C.); son and successor of Jehu; reigned (c. 816–800 B.C.); his kingdom at mercy of Damascus (*2 Kings* xiii). (2) Called **Shal'lum** (shăl'ŭm) in *Jeremiah* xxii. 11. King of Judah; son of Josiah; reigned few months only (608 or 607 B.C.); deposed by Necho (II); carried as prisoner to Egypt, where he died (*2 Kings* xxiii. 30–33).

Jehoash. See JOASH.

Je·hoi'a·chin (jē·hoi'à·kĭn). In Douay Bible **Jo'a·chin** (jō'à·kĭn). 615?–?560 B.C. King of Judah (598 or 597 B.C.); son of Jehoiakim; reigned few months only; with Judean leaders, carried away as prisoner to Babylon by Nebuchadnezzar; held captive 37 years; released by Evil-Merodach (*2 Kings* xxiv. 6–16).

Je·hoi'a·kim (jē·hoi'à·kĭm). In Douay Bible **Jo'a·kim** (jō'à·kĭm). d. 598? B.C. King of Judah (c. 608–598 B.C.). Son of Josiah. Placed on throne by Necho (II), who had deposed Jehoahaz (*2 Kings* xxiii. 34–xxiv. 7); revolted against Babylon after hegemony over Palestine passed (605) from Necho to Nebuchadnezzar at battle of Carchemish; died at siege of Jerusalem just before city was taken; succeeded by Jehoiachin (*q.v.*).

Je·ho'ram (jē·hō'răm). In Douay Bible **Jo'ram** (jō'răm). (1) King of Israel (d. 843? B.C.); son of Ahab; succeeded older brother Ahaziah as king (c. 852–843 B.C.); with Jehoshaphat of Judah, put down revolt in Moab (*2 Kings* iii); revolt against him by Elisha and his party; slain by Jehu, who seized throne (*2 Kings* ix). (2) King of Judah (d. 844? B.C.); son and successor of Jehoshaphat; reigned (c. 851–844 B.C.); m. Athaliah (*q.v.*), daughter of Ahab and Jezebel; during his reign Edom rebelled; succeeded by son Ahaziah (*2 Kings* viii. 16–29; *2 Chron.* xxi).

Je·hosh'a·phat (jē·hŏsh'à·făt). In Douay Bible **Jos'a·phat** (jŏs'à·făt). d. 851? B.C. Son and successor of Asa. King of Judah (c. 875–851 B.C.). Ruled righteously and introduced reforms; made alliance with Israel and joined Ahab in battle at Ramoth Gilead against Syrians; practically vassal of Israel; succeeded by son Jehoram (*1 Kings* xxii. 41–50; *2 Kings* iii; *2 Chron.* xvii–xxi).

Je·hosh'e·ba (jē·hŏsh'ē·bà). In Douay Bible **Jos'a·ba** (jŏs'à·bà). fl. 9th century B.C. Daughter of King Jehoram of Judah and aunt of Joash. With her husband, high priest Jehoiada, saved life of Joash when royal family was massacred by Athaliah (*2 Kings* xi. 2–3).

Je'hu (jē'hū). d. 816? B.C. King of Israel (c. 843–816 B.C.). Founder of new dynasty; soldier under King Ahab; led revolt against him; anointed king by Elisha; killed kings Jehoram and Ahaziah, driving his chariot furiously (*2 Kings* ix. 20) to the attack; seized throne of Israel and controlled Judah by destroying royal family; paid tribute to Shalmaneser III; at war with Hazael of Damascus; succeeded by son Jehoahaz (*2 Kings* ix–x).

Jehudah or **Jehuda**. Var. of JUDAH.

Je'la·čić od Bu'ži·ma (yĕ'lä·chĕt'y' [*Angl.* -chĭch] ŏd bōō'zhĕ·mä), Count **Josip**. 1801–1859. Croatian general and governor; lieutenant field marshal and ban of

chair; go; sing; then, thin; verdure (16), nature (54); K=ch in Ger. ich, ach; Fr. boN; yet; zh=z in azure.
For explanation of abbreviations, etc., see the page immediately preceding the main vocabulary.

By permission. From Webster's New Biographical Dictionary © 1980 by G. & C. Merriam Co., publishers of the Merriam-Webster Dictionaries.

NAME _____

Who Am I?

The biographical dictionary is the best place to find out basic facts about famous people. Because this reference book tries to include every famous person, the amount of information given for each person is limited. The more well known people usually have larger entries.

A. Find out why we remember the people listed below. Write what each person did and the dates he or she lived.

Person	Dates	Accomplishment
1. George Washington Carver	_____	_____
2. Grandma Moses	_____	_____
3. John B. Dunlop	_____	_____
4. Harry M. Warner	_____	_____
5. George Westinghouse	_____	_____
6. Alexander Fleming	_____	_____
7. William Herschel	_____	_____
8. Lise Meitner	_____	_____
9. Marie Curie	_____	_____
10. Luther Burbank	_____	_____

B. Name a book written by each author listed below. If more than one title is listed, write the first one.

1. Rachel Carson _____

2. Edgar Rice Burroughs _____

3. Pearl Buck _____

4. Paul Zindel _____

5. Gwendolyn Brooks _____

NAME _____

Aliases

Many famous people are better known by their pseudonyms (pen names), nicknames, or professional names. Each person below had another name. Find the entry for each person and write his or her other name. Also tell what each person was or did.

Name	Other Name	Career
1. George H. Ruth	_____	_____
2. Samuel Clemens	_____	_____
3. Jonathan Swift	_____	_____
4. Harry Houdini	_____	_____
5. Kyriakos Theotokopoulos	_____	_____
6. Mohandas Karamchand Gandhi	_____	_____
7. William F. Cody	_____	_____
8. Henry Lee	_____	_____
9. Florence Nightingale	_____	_____
10. William H. Bonney	_____	_____
11. William Jennings Bryan	_____	_____
12. Mary Ann Evans	_____	_____
13. John XXIII	_____	_____
14. Anthony Wayne	_____	_____
15. Joan of Arc (Jeanne d'Arc)	_____	_____

NAME _____

How are We Related?

Below are some famous names listed in groups of three. Find the entries for the names in the biographical dictionary. Tell how the names in each set are related.

Example:
George Washington
Abraham Lincoln
Woodrow Wilson   _U.S. presidents_

Names   **Relationship**

1. George Catlin
   Georgia O'Keefe
   Winslow Homer   _____

2. Christopher Carson
   Daniel Boone
   Sacajawea   _____

3. Warren de la Rue
   Eli Whitney
   Johann C. Denner   _____

4. James K. Polk
   William H. Harrison
   James A. Garfield   _____

5. Cole Porter
   George Gershwin
   Irving Berlin   _____

6. George McClellan
   George Patton
   William T. Sherman   _____

7. Mary Lyon
   Emma Willard
   Maria Montessori   _____

8. Mary Baker Eddy
   Joseph Smith
   John Wesley   _____

The Biographical Dictionary

NAME _____

Biographical Dictionary Test

A. Read each statement below. Write *true* or *false* next to each one.

_____ 1. The biographical dictionary lists names alphabetically.

_____ 2. A famous person may have more than one name.

_____ 3. The information always tells you if the person married and how many children he or she had.

_____ 4. The biographical dictionary lists all the books a famous author may have written.

_____ 5. A biographical dictionary contains all the facts you need for a report about a famous person.

_____ 6. The biographical dictionary will tell you if there are other ways to spell a person's name.

_____ 7. Names that begin with *Mc* are listed as though they begin with *Mac*.

_____ 8. Everything a famous person did is listed in the person's entry.

B. Use the biographical dictionary to find the names of famous inventors, authors, and political leaders. Write three names for each.

Inventors	Authors	Political Leaders
_____	_____	_____
_____	_____	_____
_____	_____	_____

106 I. M. A. Booksnoop

Unit 11

The Geographical Dictionary

Objective

The students will become familiar with the scope and limitations of a geographical dictionary.

Before You Begin

Map-reading skills are not a prerequisite for this unit. The activities direct your students to browse through the geographical dictionary looking for specific items. As in most reference book use, knowledge of the alphabet and the ability to use guide words are needed.

Motivational Riddle
A Popular Name Game

SUGGESTIONS FOR USE Use this riddle at the end of your introductory lesson about the geographical dictionary. If you are presenting the riddle to a small group, use a ditto. If you are presenting the riddle to your group as a whole, attach the riddle to the magnifying glass in the Booksnoop poster. If you plan to use this unit as enrichment, use the riddle as a challenge; then have the students find their own popular names and give the clues in riddle form.

RIDDLE
You'll find me in Arkansas, Australia, Maine, and Wales,
In Washington, twice in England, and, if all else fails,
In Vermont, New Hampshire, Oregon, and Tennessee.
Look in Minnesota, Rhode Island, and Kentucky.
My first syllable can mean the opposite of old.
My second means where ships could dock, I'm told.
   Answer: Newport

Bulletin Board
Where Is It?

OBJECTIVE The students will use a geographical dictionary to determine the correct locations of cities and nations.

DESCRIPTION The outlines of continents highlight this bulletin board. Your students are asked to match nations or cities with their continents.

MATERIALS
- scissors
- stapler
- tagboard
- pushpins
- hole punch
- overhead projector
- transparency
- pen
- paper
- world map

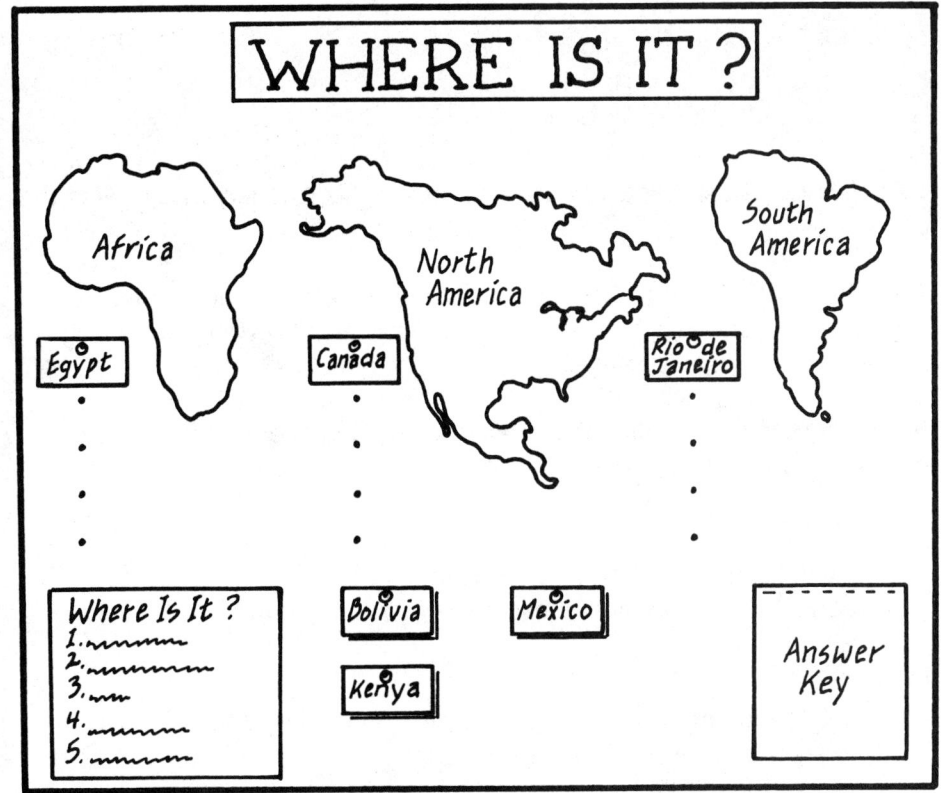

PROCEDURE

1. Choose three continents. Use the overhead projector to enlarge them for your bulletin board. Trace them onto backing paper or other paper and cut them out. Staple the continents to your bulletin board.

2. Make a list of cities and nations that are on the continents you have chosen.

3. Cut a 3-by-7 inch rectangle from tagboard for each city and nation. Print a name of a city or nation on each card. Punch a hole in each card about 1 inch from the top.

4. Place several pushpins near the bottom of the bulletin board and hang the cards on them.

5. Prepare the caption and staple it in position on the bulletin board.

6. Prepare an answer key by printing the answers on a piece of paper and covering them with a flap. Staple the answer key to the bulletin board.

7. Place a geographical dictionary at the bulletin board.

8. Print the following directions on a piece of paper and staple it to the bulletin board.

Where Is It?

1. Read the name cards.
2. Use the geographical dictionary to find the continent to which each nation or city belongs.
3. Hang each card under the correct continent.
4. Check your answers with the answer key.
5. Return the name cards to the storage pins when finished.

The Geographical Dictionary 109

Game
From Last to First

OBJECTIVE The students will use a geographical dictionary to complete the game task.

DESCRIPTION The last letter of a city is the first letter of the next city the contestants must find in the geographical dictionary. Browsing through this reference with a goal will widen your students' horizons.

SUGGESTIONS FOR USE Use this game at any time during the unit. The minimal teacher preparation needed gives this game an added plus.

MATERIALS
- piece of paper and pencil for each team
- geographical dictionary for each team

PROCEDURE

1. Divide your group into the smallest teams possible. You will need a geographical dictionary for each team.
2. Explain the rules:
    a. The team that makes the longest list of city names within the time limit is the winner.
    b. The first player makes a City column and a Continent column on the team's game sheet.
    c. You will be given a starting city name. The first player uses the geographical dictionary to find a city whose name begins with the last letter of the starting city's name. The name of the city and its continent is written on the game sheet. The game sheet and geographical dictionary is passed to the second player.
    d. The second player finds and writes the name of a city that begins with the last letter of the city the first player wrote down and passes the game materials to the next player, and so on. The last player gives the materials to the first player.
    e. Continue to find and write the city and continent names until the time limit expires. The time limit is _____ minutes.

SAMPLE GAME SHEET

Starting city: Lima

City	**Continent**
Algiers	Africa
Seattle	North America
Edinburgh	Europe

110 I. M. A. Booksnoop

Geographical Dictionary Page

Mary Esther   734   Mascara

Mary Es·ther \mer-ē-'es-tər, mar-ē-\. Town, Okaloosa co., NW Florida, 27 m. E of Pensacola; pop. (1970c) 3192.

Mary Island. See CANTON ISLAND.

Mar·y·land \'mer-ə-lənd\. **1** A middle Atlantic state of U.S.A., bounded on N by Pennsylvania, on E by Delaware and the Atlantic Ocean, on S by Virginia and West Virginia, and on W by West Virginia; 42d state in area, 10,577 sq. m. (land area 9881 sq. m.); 18th state in population, (1970c) 3,922,399; ✱ Annapolis; one of the original states of the Union, the 7th to ratify the Federal Constitution (Apr. 28, 1788).

Nicknames: Old Line State; Cockade State. *State flower:* Black-eyed Susan. *Motto:* Fatti Maschii, Parole Femine (Manly Deeds, Feminine Words). *Rivers:* Potomac, forming S boundary; Patuxent, flowing SE into Chesapeake Bay; Susquehanna, flowing across NE corner into headwaters of Chesapeake Bay. *Highest point:* Backbone Mt., 3360 ft., in Garrett co. *Chief products:* Dairy products, tobacco; livestock; fishing; manufacturing: primary metals, transportation equipment, chemicals, apparel. *Chief cities:* Baltimore, Rockville, Hagerstown, Bowie, Cumberland. See *Table of States* at UNITED STATES. Divided into the following 23 counties (for pronunciation of their names, see their individual entries):

NAME	LOCATION	AREA¹ (sq. m.)	POP. (1970c)	CO. SEAT
Allegany	NW	428	84,044	Cumberland
Anne Arundel	cen.	423	297,539	Annapolis
Baltimore	N	598²	621,871	Towson
Baltimore city³		75	905,759	
Calvert	S	217	20,682	Prince Frederick
Caroline	E	321	19,781	Denton
Carroll	N	456	69,006	Westminster
Cecil	NE corner	362	53,291	Elkton
Charles	S	459	47,678	La Plata
Dorchester	SE	594	29,405	Cambridge
Frederick	N	665	84,927	Frederick
Garrett	NW corner	659	21,476	Oakland
Harford	NE	453	115,378	Bel Air
Howard	cen.	251	62,394	Ellicott City
Kent	NE	281	16,146	Chestertown
Montgomery	cen.	496	522,809	Rockville
Prince Georges	S cen.	484	661,192	Upper Marlboro
Queen Annes	E	375	18,422	Centreville
Saint Marys	S	373	47,388	Leonardtown
Somerset	SE	339	18,924	Princess Anne
Talbot	E	261	23,682	Easton
Washington	N	459	103,829	Hagerstown
Wicomico	SE	381	54,236	Salisbury
Worcester	SE; coastal	479	24,442	Snow Hill

¹Area = land area.
²Exclusive of city of Baltimore which is administratively independent of the county.
³Administratively independent of Baltimore co. and has itself the status of a county.

History: Granted to George Calvert (Lord Baltimore) as proprietary colony 1632; first American colony to achieve religious freedom; first settled at St. Marys 1634, which was its capital 1634–94; a royal colony 1689–1715; its boundary with Pennsylvania, in dispute from 1681, settled by drawing of Mason and Dixon's Line 1763–69; first constitutional convention Aug. 14–Nov. 11, 1776; adopted Articles of Confederation 1781; ceded territory for District of Columbia (*q.v.*); invaded by Confederate forces 1862; abolished slavery 1864; adopted present constitution 1867. See BALTIMORE.

2 The southernmost county of Liberia, W Africa; 1675 sq. m.; pop. (1967e) 67,809; set up as an independent African state 1833 by Negroes from the United States; annexed to Liberia 1857.

Mar·y·port \'me(ə)r-ē-ˌpō(ə)rt, 'ma(ə)r-ē-, -ˌpò(ə)rt\. Urban district, Cumberland, NW England, on Solway Firth at mouth of the Ellen, 28 m. SW of Carlisle; pop. (1971p) 11,615.

Mar·ys·vale Peak \me(ə)r-ēz-ˌvāl-, ma(ə)r-ēz-\. Mountain, Piute co., S cen. Utah; 10,943 ft.

Mar·ys·ville \'me(ə)r-ēz-ˌvil, 'ma(ə)r-ēz-\. **1** City, ✱ of Yuba co., N cen. California, 42 m. N of Sacramento; pop. (1970c) 9353; fruit canning; fruit, dairy, and livestock farms; Yuba Coll. (1927).

2 City, ✱ of Marshall co., NE Kansas, 45 m. N of Manhattan on Big Blue river; pop. (1970c) 3588; radar equipment; poultry-packing plant; diversified agriculture.

3 City, St. Clair co., SE Michigan, on St. Clair river 5 m. S of Port Huron; pop. (1970c) 5610.

4 Village, ✱ of Union co., Ohio, 27 m. NW of Columbus; pop. (1970c) 5744; brass goods, plastics, lumber; dairy and grain farms.

5 Borough, Perry co., S cen. Pennsylvania, on Susquehanna river 8 m. N of Harrisburg; pop. (1970c) 2328.

6 Town, Snohomish co., NW cen. Washington, on Puget Sound 5 m. N of Everett; pop. (1970c) 4343; boats, shingles, leather goods; dairy farms.

7 Town, York co., SW New Brunswick, Canada, 5 m. N of Fredericton; pop. (1966c) 3572.

Maryūt, Buhrayat. See MAREOTIS, LAKE.

Mar·y·ville \'mar-i-vəl, 'mer-, -ˌvil\. **1** City, ✱ of Nodaway co., NW Missouri, 42 m. N of St. Joseph; pop. (1970c) 9970; tools, cement blocks; diversified agriculture; Northwest Missouri State Coll. (1905).

2 City, ✱ of Blount co., E Tennessee, near Great Smoky Mts. National Park 15 m. S of Knoxville; pop. (1970c) 13,808; lumber, electronic components, fabricated aluminum; limestone quarries; tobacco, corn; Maryville Coll. (1819).

Ma·sa·da \mə-'säd-ə, -'sād-\. Fortified hill on W shore of Dead Sea at S end, SE Israel; fortifications constructed 1st cent. B.C.; in 72–73 A.D. scene of final stand of Jews against Romans (defenders killed themselves rather than surrender).

Más Afue·ra \ˌmäs-ə-'fwer-ə\ *or* **Ale·jan·dro Sel·kirk** \ˌäl-i-ˌkän-drō-'sel-ˌkirk\. An island of the Juan Fernández group. See JUAN FERNÁNDEZ.

Ma·san \'mäs-ˌän\ *or formerly* **Ma·sam·po** \mə-'säm-(ˌ)pō\. Seaport city, South Kyŏngsang prov., South Korea, at head of an inlet of Western Channel 26 m. W of Pusan; pop. (1970e) 190,992; a commercial and industrial center; opened to foreign trade 1899.

Masandam, Ras. See MUSANDAM, CAPE.

Masanutten Mountain. See MASSANUTTEN MOUNTAIN.

Más a Tier·ra \ˌmäs-ə-tē-'er-ə\ *or* **Ro·bin·son Cru·soe Island** \ˌräb-ən-sən-'krü-ˌsō-\. An island of the Juan Fernández group. See JUAN FERNÁNDEZ.

Ma·sa·ya \mə-'sä-yə, -'sī-ə\. **1** Department of SW Nicaragua. See table at NICARAGUA.

2 Town, its ✱; pop. (1970e) 49,691; 5th largest city in Nicaragua; center of rich agricultural region; produces cigars, soap, leather goods, footwear, hats.

Mas·ba·te \mäs-'bät-ē\. **1** Island and province in Visayan Is., cen. Phil., S of SE Luzon; 1563 sq. m.; pop. (1970p) 492,868; ✱ Masbate. Formerly a subprovince of Sorsogon from which it is separated by Ticao Pass and Ticao I.; on the E borders on Samar Sea, on the S on Visayan Sea, and on the W on Sibuyan Sea; separated from NE Panay by Jintotolo Channel. Covered with mountains ranging from 1200 to 2000 ft. As province includes Burias I. and Ticao I. Produces sugarcane, cotton, hemp, and some rice; noted for its cattle and horses. Chief towns Masbate, Cataingan, Aroroy, Milagros, Dimasalang.

History: Explored by Spaniards in latter half of 16th cent.; long a part of Albay prov.; made separate comandancia 1846; under Americans received civil government Mar. 1901 and made subprovince of Sorsogon; created a province 1939; invaded by Americans Apr. 1945.

2 Municipality, ✱ of Masbate prov., Phil., on NE coast of Masbate I. opp. Ticao I.; pop. (1969e) 43,700; port of entry.

Mas·ca·ra \'mas-kə-rə\. Commune, SW Mostaganem dept., NW Algeria, 60 m. SE of Oran; pop. (1966c) 43,000; built on a mountain slope at alt. 1800 ft.; exports red and white wine, olive oil, grain. Importance increased when it became headquarters of Abd-el-Kader 1832; captured twice by French, 1835 and 1841, and considerably damaged.

NAME _____

Finding Your Way

Let's go traveling. The geographical dictionary can tell you about any place you'd like to go. Use your geographical dictionary to answer each question below.

_____ 1. On which page is the list of maps?

_____ 2. On which page do you find the map symbols?

_____ 3. What does the map symbol look like?

_____ 4. On which page do you find the list of abbreviations used in the book?

_____ 5. What is the first entry in the dictionary?

_____ 6. What is the last entry?

_____ 7. What place has your name or the name of a classmate?

_____ 8. How many entries begin with *Little*?

_____ 9. How many entries begin with *Big*?

_____ 10. Which is the more popular name for places—Lincoln or Washington?

_____ 11. Which color is the most popular for place names—blue, green, or red?

_____ 12. Is the place where you live listed?

_____ 13. What is another name for the Union of Soviet Socialist Republics?

_____ 14. Find the entry for Ottawa. Of what country is Ottawa the capital city?

112 I. M. A. Booksnoop

NAME _____

Clues from First to Last

Be a geographical detective! Use the geographical dictionary to solve the clues below.

_____ 1. Find the island whose name begins with *gree* and ends with *d*. It is the world's largest island.

_____ 2. Find the lake that has the largest area of any lake in the world. Its name begins with *casp*. The second word of its name ends with an *a*.

_____ 3. The name of the world's longest river begins with *ni*. What is the name? How long is this river?

_____ 4. The lowest point on earth has a two-word name. The first three letters of its name are *dea*, and the last letter is *a*. What is the name?

_____ 5. A famous volcano in Italy destroyed the ancient cities of Pompeii and Herculaneum. The volcano's name begins with *ves*. What is the full name?

_____ 6. The first two letters of the name of the world's largest desert are *sa*. What is this desert's name?

_____ 7. The world's largest waterfall has a two-word name. The first three letters are *ang*. What is its name?

_____ 8. This Pacific island is famous for its gigantic statues. The first two letters of its first name are *ea*. The last letter of its first name is *r*. What is its name?

_____ 9. This peak in South Dakota is known for its carved faces of four presidents. The first three letters of its second name are *rus*. What is its name?

The Geographical Dictionary 113

NAME _____

Get the Geographical Facts

Dig a little deeper into the geographical dictionary to find the information requested below. If the question is not answered in your geographical dictionary, write *N.A.*, meaning "not available."

A. Find and read the entry for the <u>Amazon River</u>.

1. List five facts about this river.

   a. _____

   b. _____

   c. _____

   d. _____

   e. _____

2. Who discovered this river? _____

3. In which South American country does it originate?

   _____

B. Read the entry for <u>Paris, France</u>.

1. On which river is this city located? _____

2. Who first settled in this area? _____

3. Name three things you would see if you visited Paris.

   _____

C. Read the entry for <u>Krakatau</u>.

1. What is another name for Krakatau? _____

2. Name a country near Krakatau. _____

3. When did Krakatau last erupt? _____

4. What was special about this eruption? ____

   _____

114 I. M. A. Booksnoop

NAME _____

Geographical Dictionary Test

A. Read each statement below. Write *true* or *false* next to each one.

_____ 1. The geographical dictionary has an index.

_____ 2. Entries are listed alphabetically in the geographical dictionary.

_____ 3. Only the largest cities are listed.

_____ 4. The entry may give you some information about the history of the place.

_____ 5. Many places in the world have the same names.

_____ 6. This dictionary gives information about peninsulas and large mountains.

_____ 7. This dictionary has lists of the longest rivers, the highest mountains, and the largest cities.

_____ 8. The main reason for using the geographical dictionary is to study the maps.

_____ 9. Famous explorers are mentioned in this dictionary but are not listed as entries.

_____ 10. It is not unusual for a place to have two names.

B. Read the entry for <u>Hawaii</u>.

1. How many square miles does the island of Hawaii (the Big Island) cover? _____

2. What is the largest city on the island of Hawaii? _____

3. Who was the first English explorer to visit the Hawaiian Islands?
_____

4. What was the former name of the Hawaiian Islands? _____
_____

5. When did Hawaii become a state? _____

The Geographical Dictionary 115

Teacher's Notes and Answer Keys

Booksnoop Pretest. pages 6–8

OBJECTIVE The students will demonstrate their knowledge of the uses of a library and of reference books.

SUGGESTIONS FOR USE The pretest is three pages long. The results of the pretest will guide you in preparing the appropriate lessons for your students. Students with a strong background will be able to function more independently and may benefit from a contract or learning-center approach to many of the activities in *Booksnoop*.

ANSWERS
- A. **1.** 5, 4, 2, 1, 3 **2.** 1, 2, 4, 5, 3
- B. **2, 3, 5, 6,** and **7** *should be circled*.
- C. **1.** camera **2.** Pueblo **3.** Alexander the Great **4.** antibiotics **5.** Alabama
- D. **1.** false **2.** true **3.** true **4.** true **5.** false
- E. **1.** e **2.** a **3.** d **4.** f **5.** f **6.** c **7.** b **8.** c or e **9.** g **10.** b
- F. **1.** false **2.** true **3.** false **4.** true **5.** true **6.** true **7.** false **8.** true **9.** true **10.** false

Unit I: Alphabet Sleuth

How to Be a Detective. page 13

OBJECTIVE The students will refresh their knowledge of alphabetizing and the use of guide words.

SUGGESTIONS FOR USE Make a transparency of this page and use it for reviewing or reteaching alphabetizing and guide word usage. In question A-4, bring to your students' attention the fact that two-part entries follow alphabetizing rules. In other words, *coaster* comes before *coast guard* because *e* comes before *g*. In part B, point out that a person is listed by the last name and that a geographical feature is listed by the main part of its name. *Mount Rushmore* would be under *R*, but *Mount Vernon* would be under *M* because it is a city.

ANSWERS
- A. **1.** Ala̱bama **2.** motorca̱de **3.** rhine̱stone **4.** coasteṟ **5.** microbe̱
- B. **1.** Andrew Bailey **2.** Samuel, Aaron **3.** Mount Everest *(under* E*)* **4.** Amazon River **5.** George Washington Carver
- C. **1.** before **2.** after **3.** before **4.** on **5.** after **6.** after **7.** after **8.** on **9.** on **10.** on

116 I. M. A. Booksnoop

Alphabet Clues, page 14

OBJECTIVE The students will demonstrate their knowledge of the alphabet and their ability to put words into alphabetical order.

SUGGESTIONS FOR USE Use this page as a transparency or as a student worksheet. The alphabetizing section of the pretest will help you decide how much review your students need. As a follow-up activity, have the students prepare lists of words for friends to alphabetize.

ANSWERS
- **A.** 1. c, d, e 2. n, o, p 3. e, f, g 4. m, n, o 5. t, u, v 6. x, y, z 7. d, e, f 8. j, k, l 9. f, g, h 10. v, w, x 11. i, j, k 12. q, r, s
- **B.** 1. 3, 1, 4, 2, 5 2. 4, 3, 1, 5, 2 3. 1, 2, 3, 4, 5
- **C.** 1. straight, i, n 2. Pluto, o, n 3. egoism, y, o 4. mosaic, a, q 5. Alabama, b, m 6. cycle, o, e 7. whale, a, e 8. rodent, n, o 9. victory, d, c 10. brazen, e, i

Name Sleuth, page 15

OBJECTIVE The students will demonstrate their ability to alphabetize names.

SUGGESTIONS FOR USE Use this page as a warm-up exercise for Unit 9, The Encyclopedia, or Unit 10, The Biographical Dictionary. Use the alphabetizing or names section of the transparency master to determine how much review your students need. Discuss the application of alphabetizing concepts to the telephone directory. If you need to prepare more written practice for your group, use your local telephone directory as source material.

ANSWERS
- **A.** 2, 6, 9, 1, 5, 4, 10, 7, 3, 8
- **B.** 3, 7, 10, 8, 6, 1, 4, 9, 5, 2
- **C.** 7, 6, 9, 1, 3, 4, 8, 10, 2, 5

The Detective's Assistant, page 16

OBJECTIVE The students will demonstrate their ability to use guide words.

SUGGESTIONS FOR USE Guide word use requires high-level alphabetizing skills. Most reference books have guide words. Being able to use guide words makes locating entries easier. If the guide word section of the pretest indicated your students are rusty in this area, make a transparency of this page and use it as a directed lesson.

ANSWERS
- **A.** Marianas Islands, Maria Theresa, mare, Marburg, March, margarine
- **B.** *Accept any reasonable definition.*

Investigating Guide Words, page 17

OBJECTIVE The students will demonstrate their ability to use guide words.

SUGGESTIONS FOR USE Discuss the concepts presented on the page. Explain the directions for part A. Part C may be eliminated when you reproduce this page.

ANSWERS
- **A.** 1. on 2. before 3. after 4. on 5. on 6. on 7. on 8. after 9. before 10. after
- **B.** 1. Clay, Henry 3. Cicero 5. Churchill, Winston 7. Charles I 8. Cato 9. Clark, George R.
- **C.** 9, 2, 7, 3, 6, 1, 5, 4, 8, 10

Guide Word Graduate, page 18

OBJECTIVE The students will demonstrate their ability to use guide words.

SUGGESTIONS FOR USE The activity reinforces the skills introduced on pages 16 and 17.

ANSWERS
- A. **1.** Santiago **4.** Santa Fe **7.** Scilly Isles **10.** Scipio **11.** Schubert, Franz **12.** Saxony
- B. **1.** on **2.** before **3.** after **4.** on **5.** before **6.** after **7.** on **8.** on **9.** on **10.** after **11.** on **12.** on **13.** before **14.** after **15.** before **16.** on
- C. checkers, cheese, chemical, chetah, Cheyenne, chic, Chicago, Chickasaw, chicle, Chief of Staff, chieftain, child, chimney, chipmunk, chlorine, chrome

Alphabet Sleuth Test, page 19

OBJECTIVE The students will demonstrate their alphabetizing skills and their ability to use guide words.

SUGGESTIONS FOR USE Use the test results to plan for reviewing and reteaching.

ANSWERS
- A. **1.** 6, 4, 1, 2, 5, 3, 7, 8 **2.** 1, 3, 2, 6, 5, 4, 7, 8
- B. **1.** Winchester **2.** Weddell **7.** Westchester **8.** Whitehorse **9.** West Indies **11.** Waterford **12.** White Nile **13.** Washington

Unit 2: Parts of a Book

Background Information

The typical nonfiction book does not contain all of the items listed below. However, as your more able students may ask you about them, the list is comprehensive.

Acknowledgements: The author thanks the people who made contributions to the book. Acknowledgements are usually found in the front of the book.

Appendix: Usually found in the back of a book, this section gives details that elucidate the main body of information. Charts, maps, tables, and statistics are often found in an appendix.

Bibliography: There are two types of bibliographies. The first type lists books or articles that the author used to prepare the book. The second type lists books that the author recommends for further reading. Both listings are alphabetical, usually by the authors' names.

Copyright: The copyright is the legal right conferred by the United States Register of Copyrights to the author or publisher. It gives exclusive control over the book to the author or publisher. The date of copyright and the International Standard Book Number (ISBN) are given on the back of the title page.

Dedication: This page usually follows the copyright page. The author thanks someone who or something that inspired or influenced the writing of the book.

Foreword: This section is usually written by someone other than the author and is located after the table of contents. It gives a general statement about the intent or content of the book.

Glossary: This section is located in the back of a book. It is a dictionary of special terms relevant to the book's content.

Half title page: This page precedes the title page and tells only the title of the book.

Index: This section is usually located in the back of a book. It lists items alphabetically with their page numbers. Lists of maps and illustrations may be included in an index.

Introduction: This section is usually found just before the main text. It often gives background information to introduce the content. It may serve as a preface and may be written by someone other than the author.

List of illustrations or maps: This section lists pictures, diagrams, or maps with their page numbers for quick reference. It may be included in the book's index or with the table of contents.

Preface: This section is usually found prior to or just after the table of contents. It states the author's intent in writing the book.

Table of contents: This section is located after the title page. It is a list of the sections or chapters of a book, in the order in which they appear, with the corresponding page numbers.

Title page: This page may be the first page in a book. It lists the book's full title, the author's name, the publisher, and the place of publication. It may also include the name of a translator, an illustrator, a designer, or an editor.

There Are Two Sides to Every Story, page 24

OBJECTIVE The students will become familiar with the information given on a typical title page and with copyright information.

SUGGESTIONS FOR USE This page may be used as a transparency for a teacher-directed activity or as a student worksheet. As a follow-up activity, have your students locate the title pages of the textbooks they are using. Question #7 should be discussed thoroughly. The type of information you need determines how current the book's copyright needs to be. Make your students aware that the current almanac is an up-to-date source of statistics.

ANSWERS
1. Eric Dalton   2. Land of Many Cultures   3. Fairfield Publishers   4. New York
5. Margaret Batesford   6. 1975   7. Answers will vary. It will depend on the type of information you need.   8. 0–603–02437–1

Sifting for Big Clues: The Table of Contents, page 25

OBJECTIVE The students will demonstrate their knowledge of the scope and limitations of a typical table of contents.

SUGGESTIONS FOR USE This page may be used as a transparency or as a student worksheet. Many students turn to the table of contents when the index should be used. Discuss the answers to questions B-4 and B-8 to contrast reasons for using the table of contents with reasons for using the index.

ANSWERS
A. 1. front   2. main ideas
B. 1. The Rise of the Aztecs   2. 10   3. 8   4. 2   5. glossary   6. index

Sifting for Clues: Using the Index, pages 26–27

OBJECTIVE The students will demonstrate their ability to locate information in a typical index.

SUGGESTIONS FOR USE Duplicate copies of page 26 for each student. Make a transparency of the page to use as an introduction to using an index if the pretest indicated a major weakness in this area. Page 26 is also used to complete page 27. The following concepts should be discussed: Indexes are alphabetical; there are main topics and subtopics; this index uses an asterisk to indicate an illustration, but there are other ways to do so; an item may be listed under more than one topic, and some indexes have a "see also" reference; the dash between page numbers means "through." Discuss the answers to page 26 before handing out page 27.

ANSWERS
A. 1. 46   2. 82   3. 41 and 47   4. 52   5. 42, 49, and 60   6. 64   7. 40
B. 6, 8, 3, 4, 5, 2, 7, 1
C. 1. 36, 42, 52   2. 42, 47, 58   3. 55   4. 40, 50, 42, 47, 49, 58, 60   5. 52   6. 189   7. 92–93
D. 1. alphabetically   2. The index gives the exact location of a specific item.   3. It uses an asterisk *(or italics or other device)*.   4. The dash means "through."   5. The index helps you locate details, but the table of contents tells you only the main ideas.

Teacher's Notes and Answer Keys 119

The Informer: The Bibliography. page 28

OBJECTIVE The students will demonstrate their knowledge of a typical bibliography.

SUGGESTIONS FOR USE Discuss the reasons for using a bibliography in a textbook: It tells you the references the author used in compiling the information and it gives you references for further study. Have your students locate the bibliographies in their classroom textbooks.

ANSWERS
- **A. 1.** back **2.** It can tell you where to find more information. It tells you how up-to-date the author's sources were. **3.** alphabetically by the authors' last names
- **B. 1.** Hayman **2.** Caulfred **3.** Caulfred *(The other books are primarily historical and are less likely to have out-of-date information.)* **4.** Allred, Emery, Hayman **5.** Frankfort **6.** Lernan **7.** Emery **8.** Allred, Emery

Parts of a Book Test. pages 29–30

OBJECTIVE The students will demonstrate their knowledge of and ability to use a title page, a table of contents, an index, and a bibliography.

SUGGESTIONS FOR USE Administer this test after your students have completed the activities in the unit. The ability to use an index is critical to reference-book use. Reteach if the test indicates weaknesses in the use of an index.

ANSWERS
- **A. 1.** a **2.** b **3.** c **4.** d **5.** e **6.** c **7.** e **8.** a **9.** d **10.** a
- **B. 1.** false **2.** true **3.** true **4.** true **5.** true
- **C. 1.** 37–42 **2.** 29, 32–35 **3.** 192–195 **4.** social structure **5.** 192–195 **6.** 55–56 **7.** 196–203 **8.** 30–33

Unit 3: The Dewey Decimal System

Background Information

The Dewey Decimal System of book classification is used by most libraries in the United States except the Library of Congress. Nonfiction books are arranged according to their Dewey Decimal System call numbers. All books bearing the same call number are further classified alphabetically by the authors' last names. If one author has written several books on the same topic, the books are alphabetized by title. Biographies are arranged alphabetically by the name of the person the book is about. Several biographies about the same person are further arranged by the authors' last names. Fiction books do not have call numbers and are identified by an *F* on their spines. They are placed in a separate section and are arranged by the authors' last names. Books by the same author are arranged alphabetically by their titles.

See page 37 for the Dewey Decimal System classification chart.

Where Is It? page 35

OBJECTIVE The students will become familiar with the Dewey Decimal System of classifying books.

SUGGESTIONS FOR USE Make a transparency of this page and use it to introduce your students to the Dewey Decimal System. Discuss terms that may not be in your students' vocabularies, such as *philosophy* and *technology*. If you are conducting this lesson in your classroom, make a map of your school library showing the locations of the categories. Arrange a trip to a local public library as a follow-up. If there is a large city or college library nearby, arrange a visit. Many of your students will be astounded at the materials available in a comprehensive library. A library should become a friendly place to your students if they are to feel comfortable and self-motivated enough to use it.

ANSWERS
A. **1.** General Works (references, usually cannot be checked out) **2.** Philosophy **3.** Religion **4.** Social Sciences **5.** Language **6.** Pure Science **7.** Technology **8.** Arts **9.** Literature **10.** History. *(See Looking for Clues, p. 37, for a more complete description of each category.)*
B. 4, 3, 1, 2, 5

Following Leads. page 36

OBJECTIVE The students will locate the Dewey Decimal System sections in their library.

SUGGESTIONS FOR USE This worksheet must be completed in a library. If you do not have a school library, make a list of call numbers, titles, and authors on a transparency and have the students complete the worksheet with this information. Better yet, plan a trip to a local library. Make a map of the library and use it to prepare your group for the trip.

ANSWERS *Answers will vary. Have your students share the names of the books that they find especially interesting.*

Looking for Clues. page 37

OBJECTIVE The students will demonstrate their knowledge of the Dewey Decimal System.

SUGGESTIONS FOR USE Discuss the subtopics before assigning this page. The 600s, Technology, may need further explanation.

ANSWERS
1. 400–499 **2.** 900–999 **3.** 600–699 **4.** 500–599 **5.** 700–799
6. 800–899 **7.** 300–399 **8.** 700–799 **9.** 700–799 **10.** 000–099
11. 200–299 **12.** 100–199

Remembering the Clues. page 38

OBJECTIVE The students will construct mnemonics to remember the Dewey Decimal System of classification.

SUGGESTIONS FOR USE A mnemonic device is an artificial memory aid. After the students make theirs, have volunteers read them aloud. Choose the best one and have your group memorize it.

ANSWERS
A. Mechanics prepare many Venus expeditions, never using strange jalopies.
B. *Answers will vary.*

Dewey Decimal System Test. page 39

OBJECTIVE The students will demonstrate their understanding of the Dewey Decimal System of classification.

SUGGESTIONS FOR USE Administer the test when the activities in this unit have been satisfactorily completed. Review the use of the Dewey Decimal System periodically.

ANSWERS
1. 900 **2.** 400 **3.** 700 **4.** 200 **5.** 100 **6.** 600 **7.** 000 **8.** 800 **9.** 700
10. 900

Unit 4: The Card Catalog

Tracing the Cards, page 44

OBJECTIVE The students will complete author, title, and subject catalog cards for a given book.

SUGGESTIONS FOR USE Make a transparency of this page and use it to review or introduce the three types of catalog cards. Most students will not be able to complete this activity without teacher direction. Duplicate copies of this page and have your students complete it as you lead them using the overhead projector. Make up your own book information and use this page for review at a later time.

ANSWERS

1. subject card

```
            TENNIS
   786
    G      Gonzales, Erica
              Winning at tennis. Illus by Janet Winslow.
              Brownsville Publishers 1982    176p illus.
```

2. title card

```
            Winning at tennis
   786
    G      Gonzales, Erica
              Winning at tennis. Illus by Janet Winslow.
              Brownsville Publishers 1982    176p illus.
```

3. author card

```
   786
    G      Gonzales, Erica
              Winning at tennis. Illus by Janet Winslow.
              Brownsville Publishers 1982    176p illus.
```

Tracing the Trays, page 45

OBJECTIVE The students will become familiar with the card catalog.

SUGGESTIONS FOR USE If this is your students' first exposure to the card catalog, make a transparency of this page and duplicate copies for your class. Have your students complete the worksheet under your guidance.

ANSWERS
  A. **1.** 14 **2.** 1 **3.** 9 **4.** 1 **5.** 3
  B. **1.** 4 **2.** 9 **3.** 7 **4.** 8 **5.** 14 **6.** 12 **7.** 9 **8.** 12
  C. **1.** 4 **2.** 8 **3.** 7 **4.** 6 **5.** 7

Clues in the Trays, page 46

OBJECTIVE The students will use this card catalog to find specific information.

122 I. M. A. Booksnoop

SUGGESTIONS FOR USE This activity requires a card catalog. Assign each student a card catalog tray. Have the students note that the card catalog uses guide words to assist in the quick location of cards. Instead of checking each assignment, conduct a class discussion about interesting subjects, titles, and favorite authors listed in the card catalog.

ANSWERS Answers will vary.

Clues in the Cards. page 47

OBJECTIVE The students will demonstrate their understanding of the information found on the three types of cards in a card catalog.

SUGGESTIONS FOR USE Your students should have no difficulty completing this worksheet. Use this activity as an informal pretest for the unit test.

ANSWERS
- A. 1. subject 2. 636.7 Mc 3. Mc
- B. 1. author 2. Odin and His Family 3. Robert Closse
- C. 1. title 2. fiction section 3. George Knobb

Unscramble the Clues. page 48

OBJECTIVE The students will complete the three types of catalog cards for a given book.

SUGGESTIONS FOR USE Use the transparency you made to introduce this unit as a review before making this assignment if you think your group will have difficulty.

ANSWERS

1.

```
        EGYPT
 932    Fowler, Kenneth
  F         Life in ancient egypt. Illus by Marg. Boehmer.
            Scribner Publishers 1975    164p illus.
```

2.

```
        Life in ancient egypt
 932    Fowler, Kenneth
  F         Life in ancient egypt. Illus by Marg. Boehmer.
            Scribner Publishers 1975    164p illus.
```

3.

```
 932    Fowler, Kenneth
  F         Life in ancient egypt. Illus by Marg. Boehmer.
            Scribner Publishers 1975    164p illus.
```

Card Catalog Test. page 49

OBJECTIVE The students will demonstrate their knowledge of the card catalog.

SUGGESTIONS FOR USE Use the test results to determine necessary reteaching.

ANSWERS
- **A.** author, title, subject
- **B.** 1. The Gold Rush Days 2. Sarah H. Abbott 3. 1965 4. 976.6 A 5. Goldstone
- **C.**

```
Mystery of the missing computer
Morrison, Nancy
Mystery of the missing computer. Illus. by Jerry Smith.
Weldon Publishing  1983    138p illus.
```

Unit 5: The Thesaurus

Crime Stopper. page 54

OBJECTIVE The students will become familiar with the structure of a thesaurus.

SUGGESTIONS FOR USE Make an overhead transparency of this page and use it to introduce your students to the organization of a thesaurus patterned after *Roget's International Thesaurus*. Other types of synonym dictionaries list the words alphabetically and are simpler to use. Include the following points in your discussion:
1. The thesaurus is a tool to improve the students' writing.
2. It assumes you know the meaning of the word.
3. To find a synonym or an antonym for a word, find the word in the index. Choose the meaning that fits the context of the word. Find the entry number for the meaning and turn to its location.
4. Words are listed in categories. Your word may not be a main entry, so skim the category to find it.

Sailing by Thesaurus. page 55

OBJECTIVE The students will use the thesaurus to find synonyms for words.

SUGGESTIONS FOR USE Familiarize your students with the organizational pattern of your classroom thesauruses. If you have a limited number of copies, make this worksheet an activity center.

ANSWERS *(Answers will vary according to your classroom thesauruses. These answers are keyed to* Roget's*.)*
- **A.** *Accept any interpretation of* good.
- **B.** *Possible answers are:* **1.** voyage, passage **2.** wages, compensation **3.** withstand, battle **4.** inhospitable, unagreeable **5.** capsized, upset **6.** violent, furious **7.** energy, power **8.** stationary, riding at anchor **9.** consequence, outcome **10.** prolonged, extended *(A group discussion of the individual choices would be a valuable way to complete this activity.)*

Finding the Rhyme for Us Using a Thesaurus. page 56

OBJECTIVE The students will use a thesaurus to locate synonyms that rhyme with clue words.

SUGGESTIONS FOR USE Approach this as a fun activity. Browsing through the thesaurus will make your students feel more comfortable with the reference book.

ANSWERS **1.** maim *or* lame **2.** abhor **3.** collide **4.** loquacious **5.** subdue
6. propitious *or* auspicious **7.** garble **8.** vigor **9.** sinister **10.** lurk **11.** sham
12. notion **13.** probe **14.** heed **15.** quest **16.** remorse **17.** foe **18.** gaunt
19. hue

The Thesaurus Goes to the Movies, page 57

OBJECTIVE The students will categorize words using a thesaurus.

SUGGESTIONS FOR USE Have the students locate the Synopsis of Categories section if they are using *Roget's*. Check answers through class discussion.

ANSWERS
Light — emanation, fluorescent, gleam, glimmer, glint, glow, illumination, lucence, luminary, luminescence, luminous, luster, radiance, sheen
Sound — acoustics, intonation, monotone, noise, pitch, report, sonance, sonic, soniferous, timbre, tonality, tonation, tone, tonic
Motion — activity, actuation, budge, dynamic, flow, flux, kinesis, mobilization, motor, movableness, movement, ongoing, stir, travel

Thesaurus Test, page 58

OBJECTIVE The students will demonstrate their mastery of the use of a thesaurus.

SUGGESTIONS FOR USE Administer this test when your students have completed the activities in the unit. The test requires the use of a thesaurus.

ANSWERS
A. 1. false **2.** false **3.** true **4.** false **5.** true
B. and **C.** Accept any answers that are synonyms for the given words.

Unit 6: The Atlas

Your Travel Guide: The Atlas, page 63

OBJECTIVE The students will become familiar with a typical table of contents and an index for an atlas.

SUGGESTIONS FOR USE Compare your classroom atlases with the information on this page. Make a transparency and use it to introduce your group to using the atlas. It may be necessary to familiarize your students with new terms, such as *political, physical,* and *natural vegetation*. Introduce them to the abbreviations found in an atlas. The abbreviations used on the transparency master are *C.* for "cape," *R.* for "river," *Nat'l Mon.* for "national monument," *Is.* for "island," *Lat.* for "latitude," *Long.* for "longitude," and common abbreviations of names of states, countries, and continents. Have your students explore the contents and indexes in the classroom atlases as a conclusion to your presentation.

Getting Acquainted, page 64

OBJECTIVE The students will use the table of contents in an atlas to locate specific maps.

SUGGESTIONS FOR USE Compare the atlases you are using with the worksheet. Explain any terms on the worksheet that are not compatible with your atlases. If your supply of atlases is limited, have the students work in pairs.

ANSWERS Answers will vary with the atlases being used.

Making Conversation. page 65

OBJECTIVE The students will use the index of an atlas to locate listings of cities.

SUGGESTIONS FOR USE Your classroom atlases may use a grid system for locating specific map items (for example, *A6*). If so, change the worksheet to correspond. If your atlases give pronunciations too, point out this added help.

ANSWERS *(Latitudes and longitudes are given. Consult the atlases being used for page numbers.)*
  A. **1.** 38 N, 23 E **2.** 46 N, 7 E **3.** 30 N, 31 E **4.** 43 N, 79 W **5.** 38 N, 77 W **6.** 19 N, 99 W **7.** 16 S, 68 W **8.** 33 S, 151 E **9.** 22 N, 88 E **10.** 37 N, 127 E **11.** 33 N, 44 E **12.** 22 N, 96 E **13.** 39 N, 32 E **14.** 10 N, 66 W **15.** 1 S, 37 E
  B. *Answers will vary.*

Being Neighborly. page 66

OBJECTIVE The students will use a table of contents and maps to identify countries that border given countries.

SUGGESTIONS FOR USE Your students must be able to identify borders of countries as indicated on the maps in their atlases. Have them practice finding the neighboring countries of some places not on the worksheet. Use countries that are currently in the news.

ANSWERS *(Page numbers will vary.)*
  1. Italy, Switzerland, West Germany, Luxemburg, Belgium, Spain, Monaco, Andorra
  2. Norway, Finland **3.** Austria, Yugoslavia, Romania, Soviet Union, Czechoslovakia
  4. Algeria, Niger, Chad, Sudan, Egypt, Tunisia **5.** Saudi Arabia, Jordan, Syria, Turkey, Iran, Kuwait **6.** Guatemala, Honduras **7.** Brazil, Paraguay, Argentina, Chile, Peru
  8. Afghanistan, Pakistan, China, Nepal, Bhutan, Bangladesh, Burma **9.** United States, Guatemala, Belize

Atlas Test. page 67

OBJECTIVE The students will demonstrate their understanding of the correct uses of an atlas.

SUGGESTIONS FOR USE Read this worksheet before you administer the test to be sure the major concepts have been covered.

ANSWERS
  A. *Answers will vary.*
  B. **1.** 1, 5, 3, 4, 2 **2.** 1, 5, 4, 3, 2

Unit 7: Bartlett's Familiar Quotations

Meet Mr. Bartlett. page 72

OBJECTIVE The students will become familiar with the indexing system and the form of a typical entry in a book of quotations.

SUGGESTIONS FOR USE Make a transparency of this page and use it to introduce books of quotations. Point out the use of commas in the index and the helpful guide words at the tops of the pages. The index of quotations in Bartlett's does not include authors' names. Check the books of quotations you have available and introduce your students to their indexing methods. Your students should be made aware of the footnotes used to mention quotations that are related to the one given. Discuss the use of a key word in the quotation in locating it in the index. Identify the key words *pup, dog,* and *nose* in your discussion.

Getting in Step with Bartlett. page 73

OBJECTIVE The students will construct an index from the given quotations.

SUGGESTIONS FOR USE This worksheet does not require the use of a book of quotations. Students will benefit from the indexing practice.

ANSWERS 1. 3, 5, 1, 4, 2   **2.** 5, 1, 4, 2, 3   **3.** 2, 1, 3, 5, 4   **4.** 4, 1, 3, 2, 5

Who Said That? page 74

OBJECTIVE The students will use Bartlett's *Familiar Quotations* to locate the authors of given lines.

SUGGESTIONS FOR USE This worksheet is keyed to Bartlett's. Your more able students may enjoy using the *Oxford Book of Quotations* or the *Home Book of Quotations*. Tell them that some of the quotations will not be found in those references. If you think your students are not able to identify the key word in a quotation, do this as a group activity.

ANSWERS 1. Edgar Allan Poe   **2.** James Whitcomb Riley   **3.** Aesop   **4.** Henry David Thoreau   **5.** Samuel Taylor Coleridge   **6.** Charles Dickens   **7.** Ralph Waldo Emerson   **8.** Washington Irving   **9.** Joyce Kilmer   **10.** Ogden Nash

The Case of the Interrupted Quotation. page 75

OBJECTIVE The students will use Bartlett's *Familiar Quotations* to complete quotations.

SUGGESTIONS FOR USE Your students should experience little difficulty completing this activity. You may need to define *stanza*.

ANSWERS 1. and two if by sea; And I on the opposite shore will be, / Ready to ride and spread the alarm / Through every Middlesex village and farm.   **2.** Yo-ho-ho, and a bottle of rum! / Drink and the devil had done for the rest— / Yo-ho-ho, and a bottle of rum!   **3.** In the forests of the night, / What immortal hand or eye / Could frame thy fearful symmetry?   **4.** Loved the wood-rose, / and left it on its stalk?   **5.** to forgive divine.   **6.** our fearful trip is done! / The ship has weather'd every rack, the prize we sought is won, / The port is near, the bells I hear, the people all exulting.

Bartlett's Test. page 76

OBJECTIVE The students will demonstrate their ability to use Bartlett's.

SUGGESTIONS FOR USE When the activities in this unit have been completed, administer this test. Reteach if test results indicate weaknesses.

ANSWERS
  A. **1.** true   **2.** false   **3.** true   **4.** false   **5.** false
  B. (Several answers are correct for each quotation. Accept any correct one.)   **1.** serve, stand, wait   **2.** books, tasted, swallowed, digested   **3.** fools, angels   **4.** happy, house, friend   **5.** three, secret   **6.** reward   **7.** rose   **8.** love, wall   **9.** day's, work   **10.** wishes, horses, beggers, ride

Unit 8: The Almanac

Using the Fact Locator. page 81

OBJECTIVE The students will demonstrate their understanding of a typical almanac index.

SUGGESTIONS FOR USE Make a transparency of the page and use it to initiate a class discussion about the peculiarities of an almanac index. Information about a topic is often distributed throughout the almanac. The students should have little difficulty answering the questions on the second part of this transparency.

ANSWERS
    A. 1. 687 **2.** 420 **3.** 356 **4.** 488 **5.** 712–713 **6.** not answerable **7.** 434
       8. 259
    B. 1. freight **2.** longest *or* United States **3.** inventions **4.** population

Which Department? page 82

OBJECTIVE The students will determine which questions are best answered by an almanac.

SUGGESTIONS FOR USE Use this activity to introduce your students to the almanac. Advances in technology and science, sports records, statistics of the economies of nations, facts about persons of prominence, awards given, and political developments of the year are types of information included in a typical almanac. The better known almanacs are the *New York Times Almanac,* the *Information Please Almanac,* and the *World Almanac.* Part B of this activity requires the use of an almanac.

ANSWERS
    A. *(Answers may vary. Accept other reasonable answers.)* **1.** yes **2.** yes **3.** yes
       4. encyclopedia **5.** yes **6.** yes **7.** encyclopedia **8.** yes
    B. *Answers will vary.*

Department, Please! page 83

OBJECTIVE The students will determine topics indexed in an almanac and use the almanac to answer questions.

SUGGESTIONS FOR USE Determining index topics is the key to using an almanac easily. Discuss the answers thoroughly with your group. If your supply of almanacs is limited, part B can be completed on an individual basis at a later time.

ANSWERS
    A. 1. baseball **2.** weather *or* space **3.** inventions **4.** automobiles **5.** United Nations **6.** South Africa **7.** weather **8.** coffee **9.** automobiles **10.** Saturn
    B. *Answers will vary.*

Only the Facts, Please! page 84

OBJECTIVE The students will use the almanac to write questions and answers for given topics.

SUGGESTIONS FOR USE This worksheet can become a game after it is completed. Check the questions the students have written for appropriateness first. Then divide the group into four or more teams. One person from each team sits on the answer panel. A student asks a question and the panel members compete to be the first to answer the question and earn points for the team.

ANSWERS *Answers will vary. Be sure the questions apply to the given topic.*

Almanac Test, page 85

OBJECTIVE The students will demonstrate their understanding of the use and limitations of an almanac.

SUGGESTIONS FOR USE Administer this test when you feel your group is ready. Provide more hands-on time for those students who score poorly.

ANSWERS
- **A.** 1. yes 2. no 3. no 4. no 5. yes 6. yes 7. no 8. no 9. yes 10. yes
- **B.** 1. animals 2. oil *or* petroleum 3. Lincoln, Abraham 4. lakes 5. automobiles *or* racing

Unit 9: The Encyclopedia

Finding the Keys, page 91

OBJECTIVE The students will determine the key word to use to locate the answer to a specific question in an encyclopedia.

SUGGESTIONS FOR USE Make a transparency of this activity. Include the following points as you identify the key words in part A: A key word is the main entry you would use to find the fact that will answer the question; knowing the key word in a research question will save time. For part B, explain what a cross-reference is. Point out the two usual locations for an encyclopedia's index: the back of each volume or a separate volume.

ANSWERS
- **A.** 1. barometer 2. Incas 3. gasoline 4. dodo 5. helicopter 6. knight 7. plastics 8. light 9. knot 10. immunity
- **B.** 1. b 2. c 3. d 4. e 5. a

Using the Keys, page 92

OBJECTIVE The students will find five facts about a given topic in an encyclopedia.

SUGGESTIONS FOR USE Assign one of the topics in part B to each student, or allow students to choose their own. There is a topic for each letter of the alphabet. The ability to recognize main ideas and note-taking skills are stressed in this assignment. Eliminate part D if you do not wish your students to write the paragraph.

ANSWERS
- **A.** The copyright date tells how up-to-date the information will be.
- **B** and **C.** *Answers will vary.*

Who Did It? page 93

OBJECTIVE The students will demonstrate their ability to locate information in an encyclopedia.

SUGGESTIONS FOR USE Part A reviews finding names. Part B reviews finding specific items. Since part B contains thirty items, make it an open-ended assignment by setting a minimum for the less able students and encouraging the more highly able ones to find as many as possible. The items are spread out through the alphabet to maximize the use of your encyclopedias.

ANSWERS
- **A.** 1. T 2. G 3. D 4. E 5. W 6. G
- **B.** 1. Pascal 2. Carrier 3. Volta 4. Otis 5. Ritty 6. Nobel 7. Brayton, Daimler 8. Geiger 9. Starley 10. Brewster 11. Daimler 12. Mége-Mouriz 13. Blanchard

Discover the Details, pages 94–95

OBJECTIVE The students will use the encyclopedia to research given topics.

SUGGESTIONS FOR USE This activity contains 20 research projects. Most of the projects do not require large amounts of writing. Again, topics are spread throughout the alphabet to allow maximum use of the available encyclopedias.

Encyclopedia Test. page 96

OBJECTIVE The students will demonstrate their knowledge of the scope and limitations of an encyclopedia.

SUGGESTIONS FOR USE Administer this test after the students have completed the activities in this unit.

ANSWERS
- A. 1. false   2. true   3. false   4. true   5. true
- B. 1. moon, M   2. elements, E   3. calendar, C   4. antiseptics, A   5. Alaska, A   6. plants, P   7. French and Indian War, F   8. eclipse, E   9. Marco Polo, P   10. King Henry VIII, H

Unit 10: The Biographical Dictionary

Biographical Dictionary Page. page 102

OBJECTIVE The students will become familiar with a typical biographical dictionary page.

SUGGESTIONS FOR USE Make an overhead of this page from *Webster's Biographical Dictionary*. Use it to introduce your group to the biographical dictionary. Since most libraries have limited copies of this reference, the other activities can be presented as activity centers. Include the following points in your discussion:

1. Names are listed alphabetically.
2. Refer to the *Thomas Jefferson* entry to show that information is limited to the highlights of a person's career.
3. Refer to the entry for *Jehan* to show that variant spellings are not unusual.
4. Have the students note the dates during which some of the people entered on this page lived to show the scope of the biographical dictionary.
5. Review how your particular biographical dictionaries list people whose names begin with *Mc* and *Mac*.

Who Am I? page 103

OBJECTIVE The students will locate specific information about people in the biographical dictionary.

SUGGESTIONS FOR USE If your supply of biographical dictionaries is limited, make this worksheet an activity center. Paul Zindel may not be listed in your biographical dictionary. Challenge your students to go to another reference book to discover what he did.

ANSWERS
- A. 1. 1864–1943, uses for peanuts   2. 1860–1961, paintings   3. 1840–1921, pneumatic tire   4. 1881–1958, motion picture company   5. 1846–1914, air brake   6. 1881–1955, penicillin   7. 1738–1822, Uranus   8. 1878–1968, protoactinium   9. 1867–1934, polonium and radium   10. 1849–1926, Burbank potato
- B. 1. *Under the Sea Wind* or *Silent Spring*   2. *Tarzan of the Apes*   3. *The Good Earth*   4. *The Effect of Gamma Rays on Man-in-the-Moon Marigolds*   5. *A Street in Bronzeville*

Aliases. page 104

OBJECTIVE The students will use the biographical dictionary to locate pseudonyms or nicknames and careers of famous people.

SUGGESTIONS FOR USE Many famous people are more well known by their pseudonyms or nicknames than by their given names. You may wish to introduce this activity by having the students guess who some of the people are. Make this worksheet an activity center if your supply of biographical dictionaries is limited.

ANSWERS 1. Babe Ruth or the Bambino, baseball player **2.** Mark Twain, author **3.** Isaac Bickerstaff, author **4.** Eric Weiss, magician **5.** El Greco, painter **6.** Mahatma Gandhi, Indian nationalist leader **7.** Buffalo Bill, American scout and showman **8.** Light-Horse Harry Lee, American soldier and statesman **9.** The Lady with the Lamp, English nurse and hospital reformer **10.** Billy the Kid, American desperado **11.** The Commoner, lawyer and political leader **12.** George Eliot, author **13.** Angelo G. Roncalli, Roman Catholic leader **14.** Mad Anthony, American Revolutionary officer **15.** Maid of Orleans, French national hero

How Are We Related? page 105

OBJECTIVE The students will use the biographical dictionary to determine the relationships of people.

SUGGESTIONS FOR USE If your supply of biographical dictionaries is limited, make this worksheet an activity center.

ANSWERS 1. artists **2.** scouts and guides **3.** inventors **4.** U.S. presidents **5.** composers **6.** American generals **7.** educators **8.** religious leaders

Biographical Dictionary Test. page 106

OBJECTIVE The students will demonstrate their knowledge of the biographical dictionary.

SUGGESTIONS FOR USE Administer this test when your students have completed the activities for this unit. Omit part B if you wish.

ANSWERS
A. **1.** true **2.** true **3.** false **4.** false **5.** false **6.** true **7.** true **8.** false
B. *Answers will vary.*

Unit II: The Geographical Dictionary

Geographical Dictionary Page. page 111

OBJECTIVE The students will become familiar with the geographical dictionary.

SUGGESTIONS FOR USE Make a transparency of this page from *Webster's Geographical Dictionary*. Use it to introduce your group to this reference book. Include the following points in your discussion:
   1. Entries are alphabetical.
   2. The relative importance of a place determines the length of its entry. (See *Maryland,* for example.)
   3. Show how places with the same name are listed. (See *Marysville*.)
   4. Some places have more than one name. (See *Mary Island*.)
   5. Note the types of information given: geographical and historical.
   6. Discuss the usefulness of this book in finding basic facts about a place quickly.

Finding Your Way. page 112

OBJECTIVE The students will use a geographical dictionary to locate specific information.

SUGGESTIONS FOR USE If your supply of geographical dictionaries is limited, make this an activity center. Your students should have fun with question #7. We were surprised to find places named Prizzi and Hoffman!

ANSWERS
1–9. *Answers will vary with the dictionary being used.* **10.** Washington **11.** green
12. *Answers will vary.* **13.** Russia *or* Soviet Union **14.** Canada

Clues from First to Last. page 113

OBJECTIVE The students will use a geographical dictionary to solve riddles.

SUGGESTIONS FOR USE Use this worksheet as an activity center if your supply of geographical dictionaries is limited.

ANSWERS
 1. Greenland **2.** Caspian Sea **3.** Nile River; 4,145 miles **4.** Dead Sea **5.** Vesuvius
 6. Sahara **7.** Angel Falls **8.** Easter Island **9.** Mount Rushmore

Get the Geographical Facts. page 114

OBJECTIVE The students will become familiar with entries for a river, a city, a geographical feature, and a state.

SUGGESTIONS FOR USE Make this worksheet an activity center if your supply of geographical dictionaries is limited. If you wish, have the students write their own questions about entries for others to answer.

ANSWERS
 A. 1. *Answers will vary.* **2.** Pinzon **3.** Peru
 B. 1. Seine **2.** Romans **3.** *Answers will vary.*
 C. 1. Krakatoa **2.** Java **3.** August 27–28, 1883 **4.** It was the biggest volcanic eruption in recorded history.

Geographical Dictionary Test. page 115

OBJECTIVE The students will demonstrate their knowledge of the scope and limitations of a geographical dictionary.

SUGGESTIONS FOR USE Administer this test when your students have completed the activities in this unit.

ANSWERS *(Answers may vary.)*
 A. 1. false **2.** true **3.** false **4.** true **5.** true **6.** true **7.** false **8.** false **9.** true **10.** true
 B. 1. 4,021 **2.** Hilo **3.** Captain Cook **4.** Sandwich Islands **5.** August 21, 1959